Florida Dreams Live On Through Covid-19

Patrick Grady

Published by

Global Economics

_____

in the

United States of America.

All rights reserved.

© 2022 by Patrick Grady

Cover photo: The author at the Florida Welcome Center

on I-95 south of the Florida-Georgia Line.

ISBN: 9798416120382

DEDICATION
To my cousin Tommy Walsh who sadly died from Covid a few weeks before the lifesaving vaccine became available.

CONTENTS

1	Covid Threatens Liberty as Well as Life	1
2	Florida Tackles Covid	4
3	Covid Becomes Endemic	19
4	Still a Red State	25
5	Standing Against Crime and Civil Unrest	31
6	People Keep Coming	37
7	Protesting the Crackdown in Cuba	43
8	The Economy Rebounds Strongly	47
9	A Magnet for Companies	59
10	Tourists and Snowbirds Flock Back	64
11	Real Estate Booms	73
12	Large Projects Move Ahead	78
13	Florida Dreams Live On	83
	About the Author	90
	Endnotes	92

1
COVID THREATENS LIBERTY AS WELL AS LIFE

*Those who would give up essential Liberty, to purchase a
little temporary Safety, deserve neither Liberty nor Safety.*[1]

Under the sway of the liberal media, many of my Northern liberal friends and family have expressed their repugnance of what they call the irresponsible way Covid has been handled in Florida. Governor Ron DeSantis has served as the lightning rod for much of this criticism, maybe because he is feared as a potential Republican candidate for President in 2024. Yet Northerners visiting the Sunshine State never fail to be shocked by our openness. Many feel uncomfortable and ashamed, as if naked, when maskless. And large indoor gatherings terrify them more than horror movies. But eventually even if they don't go native, they at least come to tolerate our lifestyle. Freedom can be very seductive.

Ironically, the assault on our freedoms was made in the name of science. When Covid began to crop up in the United States, little was known about this new disease and fear was so pervasive you could smell it. Even President Donald Trump, not known for his polite deference to bureaucrats, turned to the experts in Government on what to do. A White House Coronavirus Task Force was set up under the Chairmanship initially of the Health and Human Services Secretary Alex Azar and then Vice President Michael Pence. Then a star was born. Dr. Anthony Fauci, the Director of the National Institute for Allergy and Infectious Diseases, emerged from the bureaucratic shadows to take over the show purely on the force of his personality and his supreme self-confidence. After President Trump returned to Mar-a-Lago, Dr. Fauci continued to dominate Covid policy as a member of President Biden's White House COVID-19 Response Team and became the White House's chief medical advisor.

Dr. Fauci always spoke with great authority even when he was reversing himself. Masks weren't necessary, then they were. The anti-Covid vaccine prevented the vaccinated from getting Covid, then it wouldn't. The vaccinated didn't spread Covid, and then they could. Schools needed to be shut down to protect children from Covid, then they didn't. All of these about faces might have been more tolerable if they had only been delivered with a degree of humility that acknowledged that there were yawning gaps in our knowledge and that dealing with Covid was a learning process, but they weren't

Dr Fauci's changing positions were embraced slavishly by the media, both traditional and social, as scientific orthodoxy. To even question them was to risk being banned from Facebook or Twitter or even cancelled as the ultimate social pariah, a science denier. Even minor departures from the party line were verboten and had to be punished and erased.

Dr. Fauci's ultimate act of hubris was when he said that his Republican detractors were "really criticizing science, because I represent science." But by the time he made this egomaniacal statement last November, he may simply have been describing what many of his devotees believed. The dark side of this is that Dr. Fauci had become the smiling face of the new scientism challenging the freedom of Americans.

Science is not a forever settled truth like a religious doctrine, but a method of open inquiry for advancing the frontiers of knowledge. It demands a questioning and skeptical mind.

Covid-19 burst onto the world stage in late 2019 as a unknown menace. Many policies have been put forward as reflecting the science of how best to tame it. Equally as many have been scuttled, also in the name of science. While Dr. Fauci criticized others for politicizing science, he was guilty of committing the same sin. But his was worse because he used science to shut down debate, which is the exact opposite of the scientific approach and the most grievous sin for any scientist.

The objectives of policy cannot be determined by science. They must be based on the values of the citizenry. The contribution of science to policy is to provide the most effective means to obtain the agreed upon objectives. And whenever there is more than one objective for policy, trade-offs must be made. In this case, the overarching competing objectives of a policy to combat Covid are public health and a healthy economy. However, even these objectives are not entirely competing as the physical and mental health of the population is dependent on their economic well-being and their ability to participate in normal social and economic activities like school and work.

In Florida, a much more balanced approach to dealing with Covid evolved under the leadership of Governor Ron DeSantis. Notwithstanding what his critics say, it too relies on science, emphasizing the vaccine, therapeutics, and anti-virals that have been rapidly developed by the country's innovative pharmaceutical industry to the extent that this has been possible given the Federal Government's singular focus on the vaccines developed under President Trump. But, on the other hand, it also values freedom and respects people's right to make their own health and business decisions and to get on with living their lives. This applies to business owners, workers, students, retirees, indeed everybody.

My previous book, *Florida Dreams: All About the Amazing Rise of the Sunshine Mega-State*, examined all aspects of the development of Florida from the outset. This book picks up where it left off. The unwelcome elephant that tromped into the room upending the amazing rise was Covid-19. This mini tome, which is more of a long pamphlet than a book and more limited in scope than its predecessor, lays out the facts and offers my views on: how well Florida's approach to dealing with Covid has worked; how it has drawn people to Florida as migrants and visitors; how the Florida economy has fared; and how Florida's approach has become a model for other freedom-loving states. Hence the title: *Florida Dreams Live on Through Covid-19*. The amazing rise of Florida is far from over.

2
FLORIDA TACKLES COVID

Everyone was blindsided by the novel coronavirus clinically labelled Covid-19, caused by the SARS-CoV-2 virus, and originating in China suspiciously near the Wuhan Institute of Virology. Noone ever imagined that the dangerous "gain of function" research underway there sponsored not only by China, but by our own government,[2] would be the source of a world-wide pandemic, which would kill 5.7 million people worldwide, including almost 900 thousand Americans, and leave dramatic political, social, and economic havoc in its wake.[3] Florida was still riding high on the crest of an amazing boom fueled by Florida Dreamers coming to the state to take up residence. Over the decade leading up to 2019, the population had grown by around 2.7 million or over 14 percent. And current dollar GDP was over $1.1 trillion, which if Florida had been a country would have put it in 17th position ahead of the Netherlands, Turkey, Saudi Arabia, and Switzerland.

Covid Rears Its Ugly Head in China

On December 31, 2019, the World Health Organization's office in China noticed a bland media statement by the Wuhan Municipal Health Commission on their website reporting some cases of "viral pneumonia in Wuhan."[4] This information was passed on to national health agencies, including the Center for Disease Control, which immediately went on the lookout for the inevitable arrival of Covid cases in the United States. The CDC soon found what it was looking for and announced the first case on January 21, 2020.[5] It was a patient from Washington state who had arrived back in the United States from Wuhan on January 15. A subsequent CDC study revealed that this may not have been the first case and that Covid may have been introduced into the United States even earlier in December.[6]

Americans became increasingly aware of the Covid threat as news organizations reported on the official WHO and CDC releases on its spread. Ringing the alarm on January 31, 2020, Health and Human Services Secretary Alex Azar declared a nationwide public health emergency and announced President Donald Trump's bureaucratically worded "Proclamation on Suspension of Entry as Immigrants and Nonimmigrants of Persons who Pose a Risk of Transmitting 2019 Novel Coronavirus." This was Trump's controversial China ban, which was extended to Eritrea, Nigeria, Sudan, and Tanzania, as well as Kyrgyzstan and Myanmar. Former Vice President Joe Biden minced no words in characterizing it as "racist and xenophobic."[7] The ban applied to foreign nationals who had traveled to China within the past 14 days. The restrictions were extended on March 12 to twenty-six European countries. Other countries took similar steps. Worldwide travel was swiftly shut down in the face of the pandemic.

Governor DeSantis Follows Guidance and Locks Down

Fear of and uncertainty about the unknown consequences of Covid swept the nation as scary warnings of millions of deaths were disseminated by the media.[8] Florida like every other state carefully followed the guidance from the White House Coronavirus Task Force, whose frequent televised briefings turned Dr. Anthony Fauci, the Director of the National Institute for Allergy and Infectious Diseases, from an anonymous bureaucrat into a media celebrity constantly on our screens. At first, Governor Ron DeSantis implemented all the guidelines from the Task Force and the CDC, including masking, obsessive handwashing, and the sanitization of surfaces. He also imposed a compulsory 14-day quarantine period for out-of-state air travelers from areas "with substantial community spread." This included the Tri-State Area (Connecticut, New Jersey and New York)" where there were shelter-in-place orders. Starting in early March, a series of executive orders streamed out of his office declaring a medical emergency and implementing the specific steps the state government would be taking to deal with it.

Following the issuance of President Trump and the CDC's guidance "15 Days to Slow the Spread," which advised people to social distance, including avoiding gatherings of more than 10 people, Governor Ron DeSantis issued an executive order on March 17 that shut down most non-essential businesses for a 30-day period that was subsequently extended until the end of April. While Florida was put under lockdown, it was not as draconian as in most other states and in addition to the essential services specified by the Federal Government it allowed churches, child-care facilities, construction sites, and even beaches to stay open. For the latter, DeSantis was mercilessly pilloried by the national media. They had a field day running photographs of Florida beaches crowded with spring-breakers clad in their swimming suits, even stooping to use telephoto lenses to make it look like people were crammed together closer than they were. But the media failed to mention that the infections rates in April were comparable to those in California, which cracked down on beach use and construction.

Meanwhile, New York's Governor Andrew Cuomo, the fair-haired boy of the national media, was much praised for his handling of Covid and able to leverage his celebrity into a mouth-watering $5 million book contract.[9] The media turned a blind eye to his policy of requiring nursing homes to accept Covid positive patients and fell for his subsequent coverup following the termination of the policy on May 10.[10] Governor Cuomo's policy contrasted sharply with Governor DeSantis's policy of segregating elderly Covid patients in special nursing centers, twenty-three of which were established to receive patients discharged from hospitals.

Like in most other states, schools in Florida were closed for the balance of the 2019-20 school year. The Florida Department of Education and Governor DeSantis did this through an alternating series of announcements, the first of which was made on March 23.

Florida Reopens Early

Florida began reopening the state at the end of April when the shutdown was allowed to expire. A series of executive orders were issued starting with the first on April 29, which launched Phase 1 of the reopening. It allowed Floridians to resume responsible individual activity, but "avoid congregating in large groups" and "non-essential travel." It also encouraged the most vulnerable to still "stay home and take measures to limit their risk of exposure to Covid."[11] Special restrictions remained in effect in Miami-Dade County where Covid was most severe. While bars were still closed, restaurants and food establishments, retail stores, museums, and libraries were allowed to open at 25 per cent of capacity. Elective medical procedures were permitted to resume. However, gyms and fitness centers remained closed since they weren't deemed to be essential.

The Phase 1 reopenings didn't all apply in the highly urbanized counties in Southeast Florida, which had higher incidences of Covid probably due to their population concentrations. But the easing was subsequently applied by executive order in Palm Beach County on May 9 and in Broward and Miami-Dade counties on May 14.

The shutdowns-and subsequent restrictions lasted just over six months. While this seemed like an eternity to many Floridians suffering from "lockdown fatigue," it was a much shorter period than was imposed in other states, not to mention Canada.

On June 3, 2020, consistent with Federal Government guidelines, Phase 2 of the Florida reopening plan was implemented by executive order. While it encouraged Floridians to follow social distancing and safety protocols promulgated by the CDC and the Occupational Safety and Health Administration (OSHA) and some additional ones such as encouraging people not to gather in groups over 50 and the requirement for routine testing of staff in long-term care facilities, these were no longer to be enforced under Florida law. Moreover, restaurants and entertainment businesses were allowed to operate at 50 percent capacity. Pari-mutuel betting could open subject to county approvals. And personal service businesses were allowed to operate subject to Department of Health guidelines. Again, the reopening of Palm Beach, and Broward and Miami-Dade counties lagged to accommodate their special needs and they only moved into Phase 2 of the reopening plan on September 4 and September 11, respectively.

Governor DeSantis recognized that going to school was essential for children, not only for their academic education, but for participation in athletics and extracurricular activities, and for socialization. Students deprived of the opportunity to attend school fall behind academically and can even develop serious mental problems like depression that can lead to drug use and suicide. Following the science, on June 11, Governor DeSantis made it clear that he expected all schools in Florida including charter schools to open in August for in-person instruction. Faced with a temporary injunction obtained from the Second Circuit Court by the Florida Education Association staying the Department of Education's order requiring schools to reopen, the Governor got the injunction overturned by the First Court of Appeals. The schools opened as promised.[12]

Unlike in many states, in-person education resumed in Florida in the 2020-21 school year. Yes, it was subject to all the intrusive protocols like masks, social distancing, and sanitary, but then people were willing to put up with that. And even though students could choose remote learning options, most went back to their classrooms, which educators agree is far superior to remote learning on both educational and social grounds. Hence the education of Florida's students was not compromised by zoom learning to the extent that it was elsewhere. And parents of younger children were freed, from the obligation to stay home all-day taking care of their children, to work if they so choose. Florida teachers are heroes for stepping up to do their jobs despite Covid.

Covid was a learning experience even for Governor DeSantis. By September he had become even more convinced that Covid-19-related restrictions were causing "economic harm." Consequently, he lifted most of them in an executive order promulgated September 25. This order also prohibited local governments from enacting emergency ordinances to stop Floridians from working or operating a business. Henceforth, restaurants and food establishments were allowed to operate at 100 percent of capacity unless a severely circumscribed emergency order were to be imposed. And all Covid-related fines and penalties were suspended.

When vaccines started to become available in record time thanks to Operation Warp Speed, which had been launched by the Trump Administration and cut through the usual red tape of approvals by providing research funding and a ready market for the new vaccine, Governor DeSantis issued an executive order on December 23, 2020 prioritizing "long-term care facility residents and staff; Persons 65 years of age and older; and health care personnel with direct patient contact." He also allowed hospitals to vaccinate people deemed to be vulnerable. The vaccines were initially available from county health departments but, as they had difficulty handling the demand, private pharmacies were soon called on for help. The first to respond was Publix Supermarkets, which, pursuant to an agreement with the state government, gave its first shots on January 8, 2021, and quickly ramped up delivery thereafter.[13] Subsequently CVS, and Walgreen's and other pharmacies joined in, which made the vaccines more widely and easily available across the state to all who wanted them when another executive order made all Floridians eligible to receive the vaccine as of April 4, 2021.

Governor DeSantis has also emphasized the important of therapeutics like monoclonal antibodies.[14] On August 12, 2021, he announced the opening of a rapid response unit in Jacksonville to administer monoclonal antibody therapies.[15] Therapeutics is an area that the Federal Government has tended to downplay relative to vaccinations and boosters in its strategy for dealing with the pandemic. Governor DeSantis has criticized the Federal Government for buying up most of the supplies and for not making enough of them available to Florida.[16] This dispute suddenly became academic following the withdrawal of the FDA's emergency use authorization for two monoclonal antibody treatments, which forced the Florida Department of Health on January 25, 2022, to close the centers that had been established for distributing this treatment. The nub of the issue is a disagreement over whether the treatments work for Omicron, which constitutes the bulk of current infections.[17] However, the Federal Government is still open to valid criticism for not having provided an adequate supply of approved treatments like Pfizer's Paxlovid and Merck's Molnupiravir as the Trump Administration did for the vaccines.

Governor DeSantis Leads a Return of Normalcy

With the vaccine roll-out well underway, Governor DeSantis turned his attention to making sure that Floridians wouldn't be required to have vaccine passports (Executive Order 2021-81 of April 4, 2021). On May 3, he announced an end to statewide Covid restrictions and said that "there's no need 'to be policing people at this point.'"[18] To this end, he signed a bill (Senate Bill 2006), which went into effect July 1 and made it more difficult for local governments to impose mask or social distancing requirements or restrictions on businesses. But this did not prevent businesses from imposing their own requirements.

On May 13, 2021, after most people had received Covid vaccinations, the CDC issued new guidelines that "fully vaccinated people no longer need to wear a mask or physically distance in any setting, indoors or outdoors."[19] This scrapping of the mask mandate proved remarkably short lived, however. On July 27, the CDC turned around and told people to "wear a mask indoors in public if they are in an area of substantial or high transmission." On September 26, 2021, Rochelle Walensky, the CDC director, appeared on CBC's *Face the Nation* and argued, based on a flawed study, that not wearing masks in school tripled Covid risk.[20] Omicron has brought back some mask requirements. The states and territories that, as of January 26, 2022, have mask mandates for everyone are: California, Delaware, the District of Columbia, Hawaii, Illinois, Nevada (only in counties of high transmission), New Mexico, New York, Oregon, Puerto Rico, and Washington; whereas, Connecticut, and Rhode Island have mask mandates for the unvaccinated.[21] President Biden announced that the Transportation Security Administration will continue to require the wearing of masks "during international or other public travel – as well as in transportation hubs such as airports or indoor bus terminals – through March 18 [2022]."[22] This, at least, is less likely to be harmful than requiring young children and their teachers to wear masks all day long in school, which may be interfering with the children's verbal and cognitive development, not to mention the extent to which they may be traumatized by being constantly reminded of the possibility of a deadly infection if they let their mask slip under their nose or get too close to their classmates.[23]

Governor DeSantis pushed back on the return of mask mandates. On July 30, he acted to protect the constitutional rights of Floridians and parents' rights under Florida law to make health care decisions for their children by issuing an executive order requiring school districts to respect Florida laws making masking a parental choice or face legal consequences up to and including the withholding of funds from school boards not complying. When challenged by a group of parents, a Second Judicial Circuit of Florida judge ruled against this order. But this wasn't the end of the story as his ruling was stayed by the Florida First Court of Appeal pending consideration by the Florida Supreme Court. And since the panel of judges on the appeals court questioned whether the parents even have standing to bring the case, it does not look likely that the governments school masking policy will be overturned.[24]

On November 18, Governor DeSantis signed legislation protecting the rights of Floridians to make their own healthcare decisions. It banned vaccine mandates for private employers, government entities, and educations institutions and provided legal redress if their rights were violated.[25]

University and college students in Florida at public institutions have the same protections against mandatory vaccine and mask requirements under state law as students in primary and secondary schools. Public universities can recommend vaccines and masks, and most do,[26] but they cannot require them. Private universities and colleges have followed suit (except for a few that require faculty to be vaccinated). This contrasts sharply with the situation in almost all blue states and even some red states.[27] In Florida, university students are still free to have the good ole rah-rah college experience as anyone who went to the Swamp last fall to watch the Gators play football can attest.

Having survived several waves of Covid including the Delta variant in late summer and early fall of 2021, Florida was confronted in late November with the onset of the Omicron variant of Covid, which originated in South Africa and precipitated travel bans from Southern Africa and other countries where the virus has spread. The media fanned the flames of hysteria, but it's true that Omicron may not be as benign as portrayed by some.[28]

President Biden and Dr. Fauci refused to rule out further lockdowns like we had in early 2020. However, on December 2, 2021, when President Biden announced a package of new measures to combat the Delta and Omicron variants of Covid this winter, it did not include renewed lockdowns.[29] There is a growing body of evidence that lockdowns only have a negligible effect on Covid deaths, but at a cost of great economic and social damage.[30] But who knows what is to come? It was not reassuring to hear the President joke about Dr. Fauci being the President.[31]

Governor DeSantis has made the commitment that at least "In Florida, we will not let them lock you down, we will not let them take your jobs, we will not let them harm your businesses, we will not let them close your schools."[32] This is based on the Governor's view that Covid is proving impossible to fully irradicate and has become endemic. Dr. Fauci and other experts have also expressed this view although with less force.[33] If Covid can't be eliminated, we indeed must learn to live with it and get on with our lives. That is exactly what Floridians have been doing under the capable leadership of Governor Ron DeSantis.

Florida's Anti-Covid Policies Among Least Restrictive

The Federal Government controls aspects of Anti-Covid policy. For instance, measures impacting public transportation, such as masking requirements on airlines and trains, are imposed by the Transportation Security Administration, and certain restrictions on travelers like vaccination requirements or bans from certain countries are enforced at the international border by Customs and Border Protection. The CDC and other Federal Agencies also issue recommendations and guidelines on a wide variety of Covid-related public health issues. However, it's the state governments that have the responsibility for translating them into action and dealing most directly with the pandemic. A full understanding of Anti-Covid policies requires a detailed understanding of the measures taken by state governments. In a federal system, these policies and measures differ from one state to another.

At first glance, the most important policies pursued by the Florida Government seem much less restrictive than the policies imposed in the large Democratic states in the Northeast and on the West Coast. However, proving this requires much more comprehensive and systematic information on Anti-Covid policies across the country than has been presented herein thus far.

Fortunately, this is exactly what has been compiled and is available on a continually updated basis from the Oxford COVID-19 Government Response Tracker, produced at the Blavatnik School of Government, University of Oxford.[34] While this ambitious project requires a lot of judgements to be made and leaves much room for quibbles over details and methodology, it is a remarkable tour de force that provides researchers with a well-documented data source that not only covers the United States and all the states, but most of the rest of the world, including many subnational jurisdictions as well. It is a veritable treasure trove of information on the global government policy response to Covid.

The Covid Tracker includes four indexes that measure distinct types of government policy responses to Covid. The one of most relevance to the question at hand is the Stringency Index for the government policy responses in all the states including, of course, Florida. For the various states, this index "records the strictness of 'lockdown style' closure and containment policies that primarily restrict people's behavior."[35] It is based on nine ordinal components quantifying the degree of: school closures; workplace closing; the cancelation of public events; restrictions on gatherings; the closing of public transport; stay at home requirements; restrictions on internal movement; international travel controls; and public information campaigns. The international and some of the domestic travel controls component of the index reflect Federal Government policy, but the other components are primarily state responsibilities. The index itself is a simple average of its components which are scaled between zero and 100.

The Oxford Stringency Index shows that Anti-Covid policies in Florida were tightened dramatically in March and April 2020 when the economy was locked down for six weeks pursuant to Governor DeSantis's executive order of March 17, 2020 (Chart 1). The index then fell after his executive order of September 23, 2020, lifting many of the remaining restrictions and again in April and May 2021 when additional restrictions were lifted. By January 23, 2022, the Stringency

Index had fallen to 26.85, which is much lower than for the other mega-states of California (42.59) and New York (38.59) and slightly higher than for Texas (25.0). The index would be the same as for Texas except for masking requirements being imposed contrary, to state policy, on employees and visitors by school boards in the Democratic-voting counties of Alachua, Broward, Duval, and Miami-Dade. Nevertheless, according to the Stringency Index, Florida is among the states with the lowest degree of restrictiveness and California and New York are among the most restrictive.

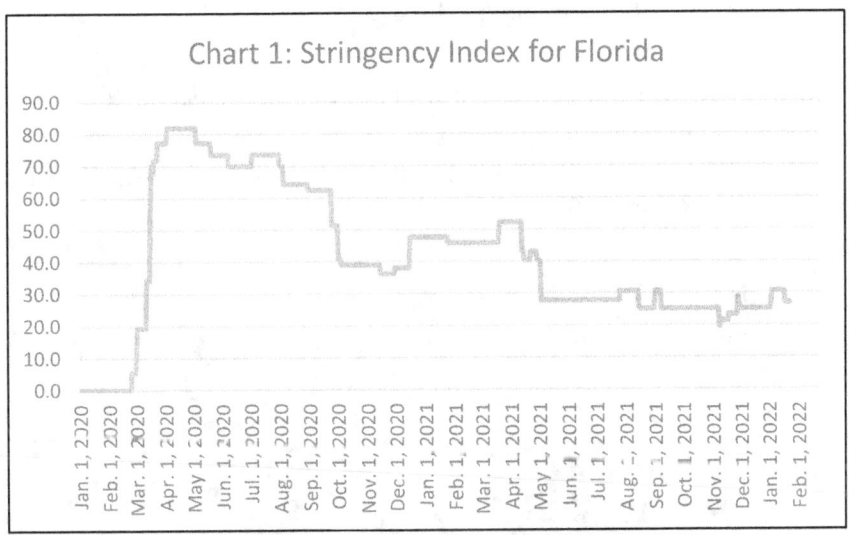

Source: Oxford COVID-19 Government Response Tracker, Blavatnik School of Government, University of Oxford, January 28, 2022.[36]

To make comparisons among states, it is best to use averages over time rather than point of time estimates to capture the full extent of the restrictive policies imposed. Consequently, averages were calculated for all the states over the 2020 and 2021 years for the available data as of December 4. Missing values for days were not counted in the averages as was done by the Oxford University researchers in their own studies.

Taking averages of the daily Stringency Indices, Florida had less restrictive policies than most of the other states in 2020 (Chart 2). The average Stringency Index for Florida was 49.9, which placed it well below New York, which was 61.8, and California (55.7), but above Texas (48.5). Florida's rank out of the 50 states and the District of Columbia was 28th, which means 27 states had more restrictive policies. A close inspection of Chart 1 shows that the Northeastern and West Coast states tended to have the most restrictive policies and the Southern, Midwestern, and Western states tended to have the least restrictive. It also shows that Democratic states had much more restrictive policies than Republican states. New Mexico and Hawaii are extreme examples as is Maine and New York. This connection between political party in power and restrictiveness of policy is confirmed by the average Stringency Index which was 56.1 in 2020 for the 16 states controlled by Democrats and 46.8 for those 23 states under Republicans.[37]

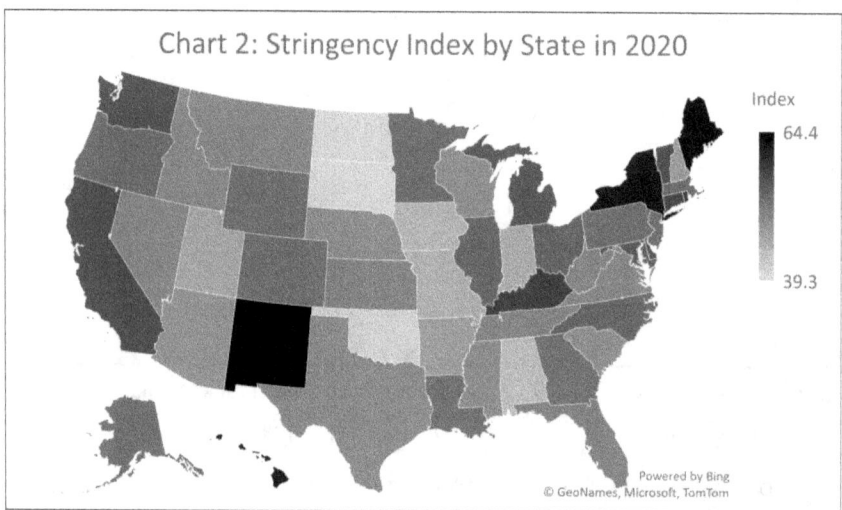

Source: Calculation on data from the Oxford COVID-19 Government Response Tracker, Blavatnik School of Government, University of Oxford, December 4, 2021.

According to the average of the Stringency Index, policy became less restrictive across the country in 2021 as the vaccine and more therapeutics became available making people less worried about Covid and as states started to open (Chart 3). Florida was ahead of the pack, especially most of the states in the Northeast and on the West Coast. The average Stringency Index in Florida fell to 34 in

2021. This put Florida in 50th position among the states and the District of Columbia. Only Iowa had a slightly lower Stringency Index reading at 33.8. Florida was well below New York (49.6) and California (49), and even below Texas (39.9), another Republican state that prides itself in its non-interventionist government. Again, the pattern shows the Democratic states in the Northeast and on the West Coast had the most restrictive policies. Hawaii, a Democratic state, won the dubious honor of having the most restrictive policies with a Stringency Index of 61.1. The non-Democratic state with a high Stringency Index, is Louisiana, but it has a Democrat Governor. Florida had a lower average Stringency Index than other states, except for Iowa, many of which had lower values of the Stringency Index in November 2021, because it eliminated restrictions more quickly than other states. Using the Ballotpedia classification of states again, the average Stringency Index was 45.7 in 2021 for the 16 Democrat-run states and 38.3 for the 23 Republican, representing a significantly lower level of stringency for GOP run states.

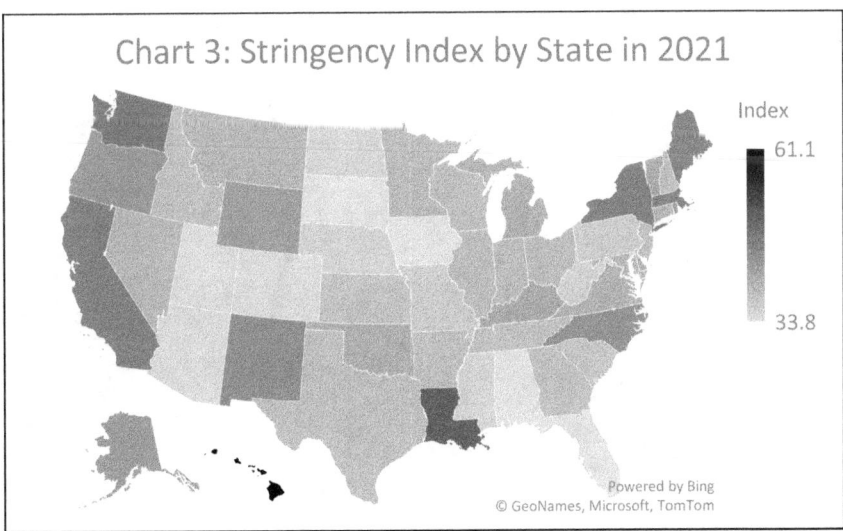

Source: Calculation on data up until the end of November 2021 from the Oxford COVID-19 Government Response Tracker, Blavatnik School of Government, University of Oxford, December 4, 2021.

It wasn't me that first noted the divergence in policies between Republican and Democratic states. A study done by the Oxford group using the same data source up to the end of April 2021 concluded that "While divergence in stringency lessened as more states moved toward phases of reopening, Northeastern and Democrat-led states maintained the most stringent policies, while Midwestern, Southern and Republican-led states making [sic] up the states with the least stringent ongoing responses."[38] This conclusion holds up even using the revised data extending out to November 2021, which is displayed in Charts 2 and 3 above.

The higher stringency in Democratic states is not over yet. In December 2021 California reimposed an indoor mask mandate. It joins eleven other states and the District of Columbia, all of which are governed by Democrats.[39]

3
COVID BECOMES ENDEMIC

Florida was hit quicker and harder than most states by Covid because of the large number of people coming from all over the country and the world who visit Florida and bring the virus with them from other places where there are outbreaks. There was a special concern in the spring of 2020 when Covid was much higher in the Northeast and winter vacationers were making their annual pilgrimage to Florida for the sunny weather and beaches. Fear of Covid was much greater in those days before we began to understand what we were up against and before we had vaccines and effective therapeutics to combat it.

Covid Ebbs and Flows

Covid appears to have washed over Florida in waves like the national pattern (Chart 4). It gathered momentum in early April, while we were all hunkered down wearing masks and social distancing even outside but remained at a low level. What was frightful, though, was the high number of deaths that followed the new cases with a lag. It became downright scary in the early summer of 2020 when cases and deaths spiked. Covid was clearly much more lethal, at least then, than other contagious diseases like influenza and pneumonia. Cases and deaths fell off through the fall, but then jumped sharply starting in November through January before dropping steadily through mid-summer of 2021 as the vaccine rollout proceeded. But Covid was not yet done with Floridians. Another even stronger wave was building in July driven by the nasty Delta variant. It pushed Covid cases and deaths to new highs in August and September with the majority of those affected being the unvaccinated as the vaccines proved effective. After peaking, cases and deaths fell off precipitously. Perhaps this resulted from the achievement of herd immunity since most people had either been fully vaccinated or had developed natural immunity from having had the disease.

But this more felicitous situation didn't last long before along came the Omicron variant, afflicting even the vaccinated and those who had already had Covid as well as the unvaccinated, although fortunately not nearly to the same degree. While this variant was much more contagious (and the number of cases may be grossly underestimated since a much smaller proportion of those who get the disease present themselves for medical attention particularly if they are vaccinated), it was much less lethal as can be seen by the smaller spike in deaths relative to the number of cases that accompanied it. Nevertheless, it did drive up hospitalization, especially of the unvaccinated, because of its much higher incidence.[40] As of January 31, 2022, 84 percent of ICU beds in Florida hospitals where occupied but this was only 1 percentage-point above the national average, and it was not all by Covid patients.[41] This is a high level of demand on ICU capacity.

Given Omicron's lesser severity, it does not give rise to the same degree of fear and loathing as the original killer variant. Moreover, now at the time of writing (January 26, 2022In), it too seems to be receding. But there always is the risk that the emergence of new variants and declines in immunity over time will drive the case numbers back up again. That is where the new therapeutics come in to keep hospitalizations and deaths down.

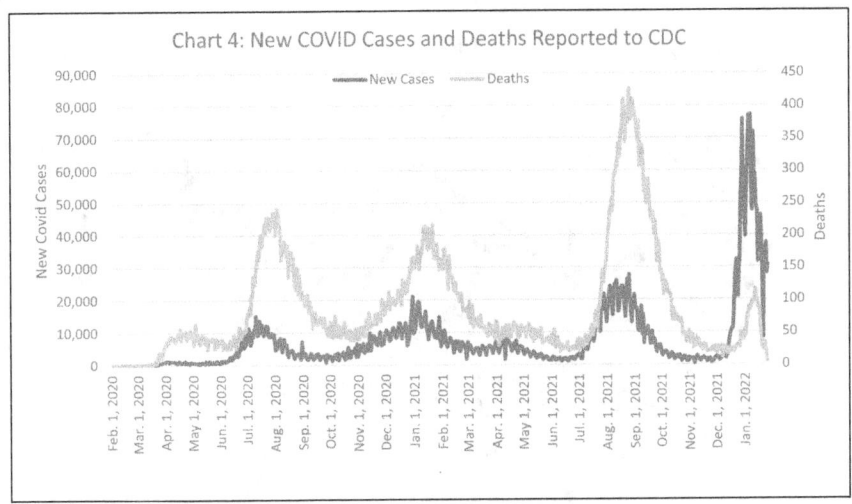

Source: CDC, Daily Trends in Number of Covid-19 Cases and Deaths.[42]

Floridians Aren't Anti-Vaxxers

Vaccination rates in January 2022 were slightly above the national average (Chart 5). In Florida 75.1 percent of the population over eighteen was fully vaccinated which was slightly above the 74 percent average rate for the United States. And the Florida vaccination rate was above the 70.4 percent in Texas, but almost 10 percentage points below the 84.5 per cent in New York State and a little below the 79.2 percent in California. Thus, Florida is not the den of anti-vaxxers that many in the media would like the public to believe.[43] However, it is true that Republican states have lower percentage vaccination rates than Democrat. On average only 66.5 percent of the population over eighteen in Republican states were fully vaccinated as of January 29, 2022, compared to 78.2 percent in Democratic states. The states with divided governments were in the middle with a 70.8 percent vaccination rate, which is incidentally below Florida.

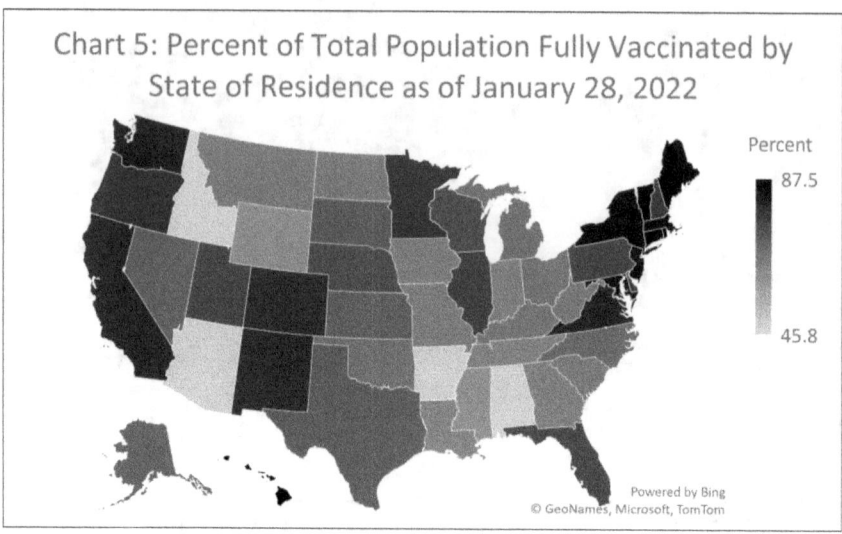

Source: CDC, Covid Data Tracker, January 29, 2022.[44]

Florida Has Had a Relatively Higher Number of Covid Cases

Florida has had a relatively high rate of Covid cases over the two years that Covid has plagued the world. Based on the total number of cases as a percentage of the population up to January 28, 2022, Florida had the eighth highest Covid rate among the states (Chart 6). This represented 25.7 percent of the population. It was higher than the 20.1 percent recorded in California and the 21.3 percent in Texas but about the same as the 25.3 percent in New York. As a rule, there were higher rates of Covid infection in Republican than Democratic states, reflecting the lower level of enforcement of restrictive Anti-Covid measures and lower vaccination rates on average. On the positive side, the higher proportion of people who had had Covid in Florida means a higher rate of natural immunity, which would, at least partially, offset the higher vaccination rates in the Democratic states in the Northeast and on the West Coast going forward.

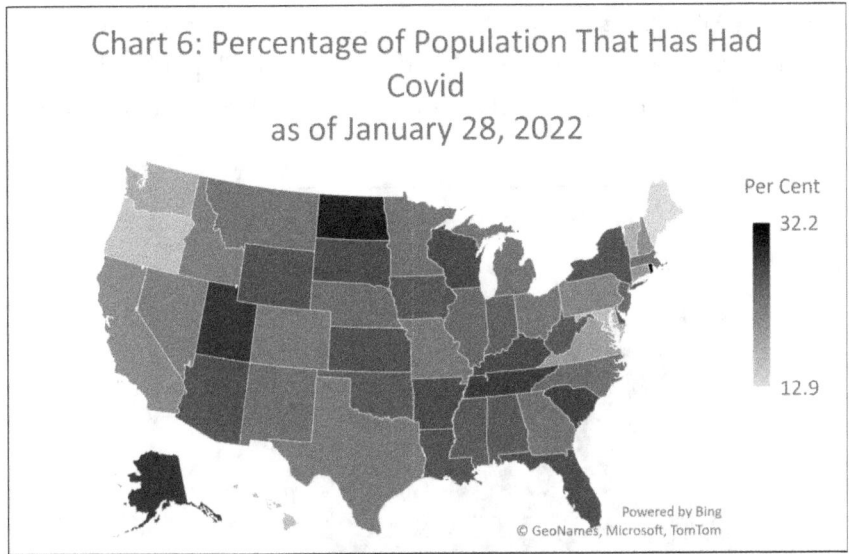

Source: Worldometers from CDC.[45]

But Not as Many People Died as in New York

Florida looks better in comparison to other states when deaths from Covid are considered (Chart 7). With 64,640 Covid deaths or 3,010 per million of population as of January 28, 2022, Florida ranked 18th in the number of deaths relative to population. While this was well ahead of California, which only experienced 2,025 deaths per million population, and more than in Texas, which only had 2,740 deaths per million, it was less than New York's 3,337 per million. Florida's lower death rate is even more impressive in relation to New York's when the much higher number of seniors who are more vulnerable living in Florida is taken into account. This better performance can be attributed to Governor DeSantis's policy of segregating elderly Covid victims rather than sending them back to their own facilities where they could spread Covid as was done by Governor Cuomo in New York. Florida also had less deaths than New Jersey, which had 3,526 per million.

On average, it is true that Republican states experienced more Covid deaths per million than Democrat – 2,838 versus 2,293, with states with divided governments in the middle at 2,418. But this is not as big of a difference as you would have thought given the acrimony with which the less restrictive policies in Republican states have been attacked by some Democrats, Florida being the main case in point.

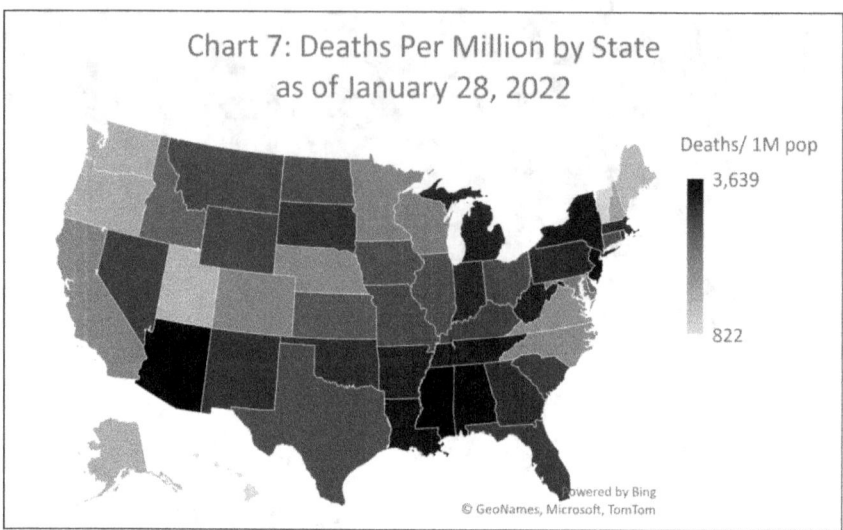

Source: Worldometers from CDC.

Living With Covid Seems Unavoidable

The approaches of Governor DeSantis and President Biden are poles apart on dealing with Covid. Governor DeSantis wants us to get on with our lives while President Biden has warned that "we are looking at a winter of severe illness and death for the unvaccinated, for themselves and their families and the hospitals they'll soon overwhelm."[46] It has proved impossible to eliminate all cases of Covid and avoid all deaths even in the states that have imposed the most restrictive policies. The key question is: how long can we afford to continue our obsession with Covid and at what cost to ourselves and our children?

4
STILL A RED STATE

Ron DeSantis Elected Governor in 2018

A</sub>lthough nobody knew it at the time, the 2018 Florida midterm election was the key event determining how Florida would deal with Covid. It put Ron DeSantis, a Republican U.S. Congressman representing Florida's Sixth Congressional District on the northeast coast of Florida south of Jacksonville, in the Governor's mansion. His victory over Andrew Gillum, the Democrat mayor of Tallahassee, was by a slim margin. And it only came after a mandatory machine recount that saw DeSantis' advantage dwindle to only 32,463 votes out of 8,220,561 cast or 0.4 percent. It took two weeks after the election before DeSantis was certified as the 46th Governor of Florida.

Even though DeSantis squeaked into office, he brought with him a secure mandate to govern. The Cabinet was firmly in his corner with three of four elected statewide officers being Republicans. This included: the Lieutenant Governor Jeanette Nuñez; Attorney General Ashley Moody; and Chief Financial Officer Jimmy Patronis. The only Democrat elected to statewide office was Commissioner of Agriculture and Consumer Affairs Nicole "Nikki" Fried. DeSantis also kept control of the state legislature with a 74-46 advantage in the

State House and 23-17 in the State Senate, which gave him the votes needed to get his legislative agenda passed.[47]

Ron DeSantis couldn't have been more different from his Democrat opponent Andrew Gillum. After graduating from Yale and earning a law degree from Harvard University, he was commissioned as an officer in the Navy, and assigned to the Judge Advocate General's Corps (JAG). Subsequently serving as the Legal Advisor to the SEAL Commander, Special Operations Task Force-West in Fallujah, he became an Iraq war veteran with the medals to prove it.[48]

Ron DeSantis is a conservative Republican. He was a Tea Partyer and a three-term Freedom Caucus Congressman. In contrast, Andrew Gillum is a so-called Progressive Democrat, who had the support of Black Lives Matter when he ran for Governor, and who drifted further leftward as the progressive forces became more dominant in the Democrat Party during the period leading up to the 2020 election and thereafter.[49]

Scandals emerged during Gillum's gubernatorial run. A criminal investigation of municipal corruption in Tallahassee looked like it might damage Gillum's campaign, but never did much harm.[50] However, after the election in early March 2020, another scandal broke. Gillum was found by police in a hotel room in South Beach with three other men, including a "hunky gay escort," who appeared to have overdosed on drugs.[51] The police report said that three baggies of what was thought to be crystal methamphetamine was on the bed and floor.[52] In addition, after this incident Gillum came out of the closet as bisexual on the *Tamron Hall Show*, which raises further suspicions about what the men may have been doing in the hotel room.[53] The character of the two men who ran for Governor is evidently as disparate as their politics.

The National Election of 2020

Despite Covid and the continuing immigration from blue states and Latin America and the Caribbean, Florida has defied the odds and become even redder. Despite losing the vote and the electoral college at the national level, Donald Trump picked up 1,050,845 more votes in 2020 than in 2016 in his new home state (Chart 8) and increased his margin from 49 percent to 51.2 percent (Chart 9). The total vote in Florida increased substantially because of the greater level of turnout induced by the hotly contested nature of the election.

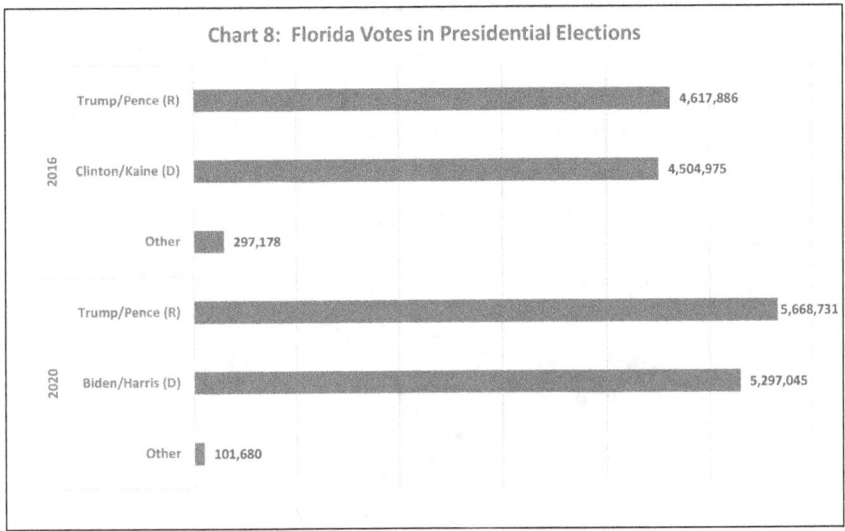

Source: Florida Department of State.

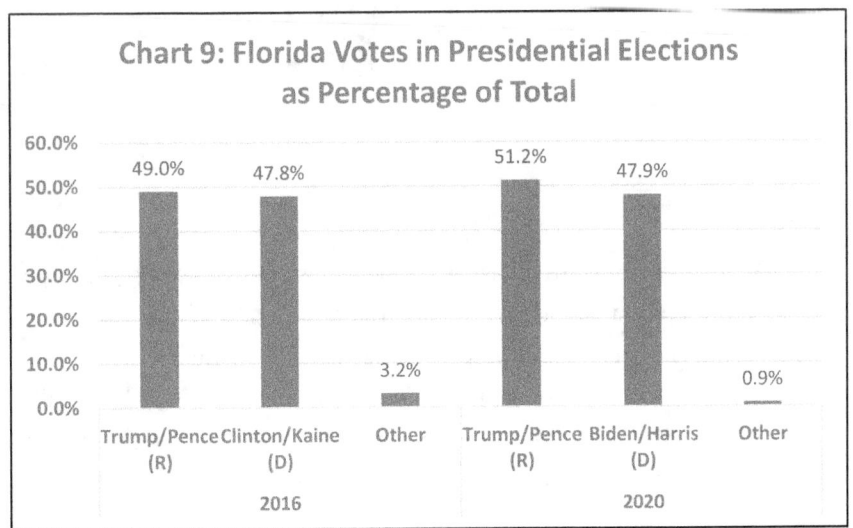

Source: Florida Department of State.

Trump's support was concentrated outside the major urban areas, but even though he lost in Miami-Dade, the state's largest county where the Hispanic vote predominates, he still got more support than in 2016, in part because his hardline anti-socialism position resonated with Cuban and Venezuelan Americans who knew first-hand about the situation in socialist/communist countries. Biden only won in twelve counties by progressively smaller margins: Gadsden, Broward (Fort Lauderdale), Leon (Tallahassee), Alachua (Gainesville), Orange (Orlando), Osceola, Palm Beach, Miami-Dade, Hillsborough (Tampa), Duval (Jacksonville), Seminole, and Pinellas (St. Petersburg). Trump won the other fifty-five counties, hands down in most by overwhelming margins (Chart 10).

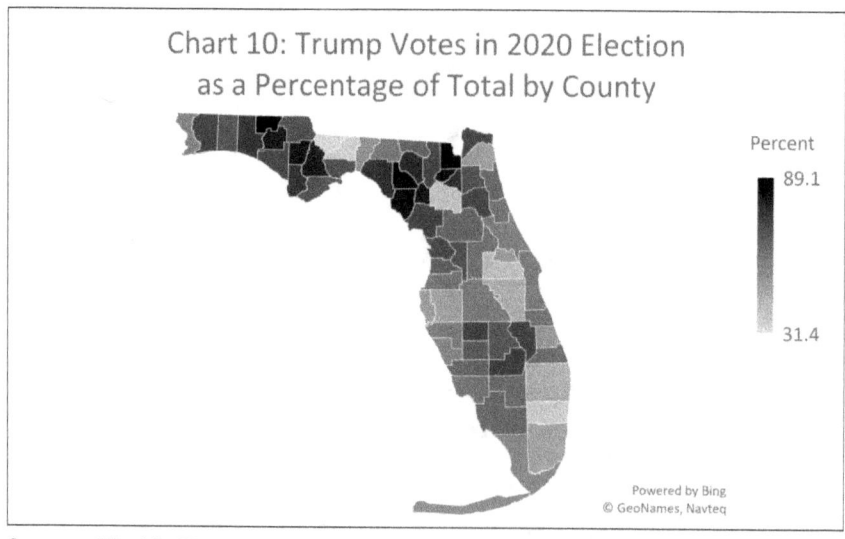

Source: Florida Department of State.

Two counties in the Panhandle were at opposite poles of Florida voting. Holmes county bordering on Alabama where nine out of every ten people are white voted 89.1 percent for Trump and only 10.2 percent for Biden, whereas Gadsden County, which is Florida's only majority Black County with 56 percent African American, voted 68 percent for Biden and only 31.4 percent for Trump.

The Trump coattails and the Cuban American community helped the Republicans to take two House seats in Miami-Dade in Hispanic districts that had been lost in the 2018 mid-term election. In Florida's-26th district, Cuban American Carlos A Giménez, the former Mayor of Miami-Dade, defeated incumbent Debbie Mucarsel-Powell, an Ecuadorian American. In Florida's 27th, Maria Elvira Salazar, a well-known Cuban American, Spanish language television journalist, beat Donna Shalala.

It wasn't only in the U.S. House that the Republicans gained seats in Florida. The Republicans solidified their hold on the state legislature winning five seats in the State House of Representatives and one in the State Senate (Chart 11). With Ron DeSantis as Governor until 2022, Marco Rubio serving as Senator until 2022, and Rick Scott till 2024, Florida doesn't look like a state that is trending purple. However, ex-President Trump, who has taken up residence in Mara Lago will be a bigger than life presence on the Florida political scene and perhaps even a wild card that could disrupt this balance.

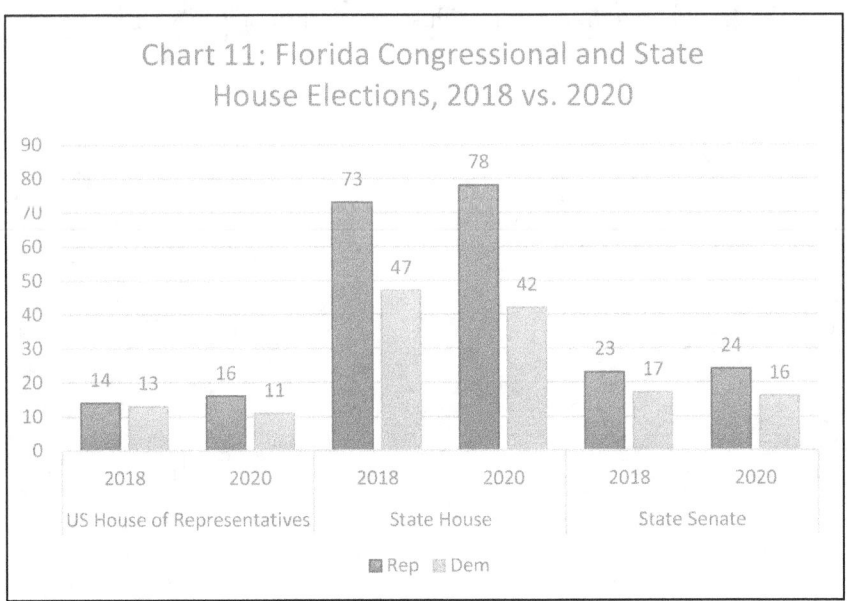

Source: Florida Department of State.

Red and Blue Cleavage on Covid Explains Florida's Anti-Covid Policies

That Florida is still a red state explains much about our attitudes to Covid. A new poll conducted by Morning Consult for the *New York Times* is very revealing.[54] It shows that young people are more worried than old people about Covid and the vaccinated more than the unvaccinated, even though the young and the vaccinated are much less seriously affected by the disease. It also shows that Republicans are less willing than Democrats to make changes in their normal activities because of the Omicron variant of Covid (30 percent versus 65 percent). And Republicans are also much less worried than Democrats about their children catching Covid at school (49 percent versus 83 percent). And, most telling of all, Republicans are less supportive of switching students to online learning (29 percent versus 65 percent). Judging from this poll, the policies for dealing with Covid in a red state like Florida illustrate democracy at work.

5
STANDING AGAINST CRIME AND CIVIL UNREST

The George Floyd Riots Come to Florida

Following the killing of George Floyd by a police officer in Minneapolis on May 25, 2020, protests led by Black Lives Matter started in that city and quickly spread across the country. On many occasions, it did not take much to turn the peaceful protests violent, especially after dark. And many of the country's major cities were shaken to their very cores with rioting, looting, arson, and even the murder of police officers. The worst examples were in Minneapolis, Seattle, Portland, Los Angeles, Chicago, Memphis, Louisville, Atlanta, New York, Philadelphia, and Washington D.C. where sympathetic city governments turned their back on their police departments and responded to BLM's demands to defund the police. To make the situation worse, isolated instances of police excesses kept popping up in different cities and kept the pot boiling for many months all over the country. All this civil unrest and these demonstrations occurred during a period when the country was supposed to be locked down because of Covid, and when many people were released from jail because of Covid.

An organization called Property Claim Services (PCS), which tracks insurance claims, estimated that the vandalism and looting that followed the death of George Floyd over the period from May 26 to

June 8, 2020, cost the insurance industry between $1 and $2 billion, making them the costliest protest demonstrations in recent history.[55] People should not be surprised to see the costs of the required increases in insurance premiums added to the prices of goods and services they buy, including property insurance.

As a large diverse, urbanized state with a large Black population, Florida wasn't immune from these developments. Black Lives Matter demonstrations did break out across Florida.[56] But apart from a few episodes of violence in Jacksonville, Tampa, and Miami, the protests were peaceful and didn't result in much property damage unlike in the rest of the country.

The protest demonstrations in Florida didn't spiral out of control like elsewhere because the state and local governments took a tough stand, which, although it respected the First Amendment rights of people to protest, didn't tolerate a breakdown in law and order. The Florida Government didn't sit around fiddling when fires burned as in some other states.

A protest in Miami on May 30, 2020, degenerated under cover of darkness into an attack on the Bayside Marketplace, a popular tourist destination. Stores were looted and ransacked. Meanwhile, nearby at the Miami Police Headquarters, rocks and bottles were thrown at police by protestors. Several cars, including police cars, were set on fire. Police finally had to resort to firing tear gas and rubber bullets to break up the unruly crowd. In the aftermath, there was no talk of defunding the police from Miami-Dade County mayor Carlos A. Giménez. Instead, he declared a local state of emergency and, to nip disorder in the bud, imposed a 7-day 10 p.m. curfew, which was subsequently extended. The Cuban American politicians who run Miami are tough and respond quite differently from the progressives in office in most big U.S. cities. They were effective at shutting down the violence before it got out of hand.[57]

On June 1, Governor DeSantis mobilized seven hundred National Guard troops to support local law enforcement in handling the protests. To make it clear where he stood, he issued a strong statement saying that "Florida has zero tolerance for violence, rioting and looting. George Floyd's murder was appalling, and the Minnesota perpetrators need to be brought to justice, but this was not allowed to be used as a pretext for violence in our Florida communities."[58]

Increase in Crime in 2020

With Covid raging, prisoners were released from jail across the country. Protests provided a perfect cover for lawbreakers. There was an increase in crime across the country. The increase in 2020 in the rate of violent crime in Florida at 5.4 was small and below the increase in the U.S. rate of 17.7 (Chart 12). However, it was slightly higher than in California (-0.1) and New York (2.8), but lower than Texas (24.7).

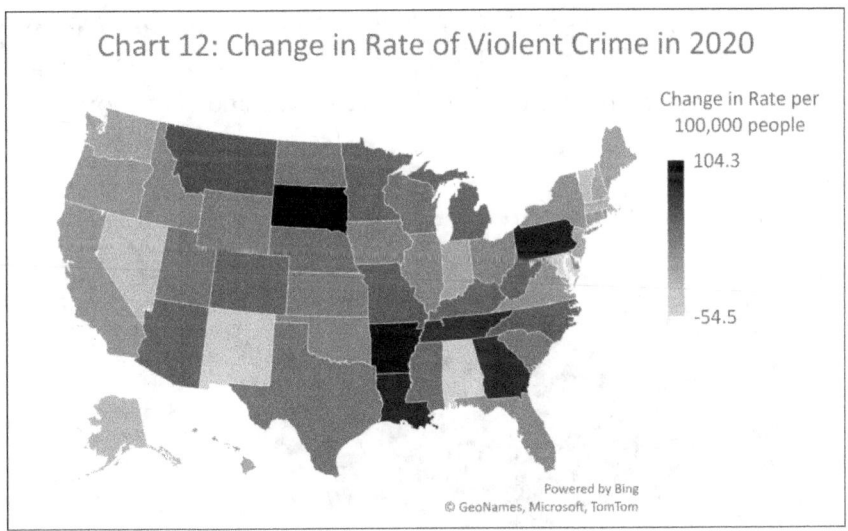

Source: FBI Crime Data Explorer.[59]

Florida looks better in relation to the increase in the rate of homicides in 2020 (Chart 13). It only had a relatively slight increase of 0.7 per 100,000 people, which was half the 1.4 increase in the U.S. as a whole and less than the 1.3 increase in both California and New York and the 1.7 increase in Texas.

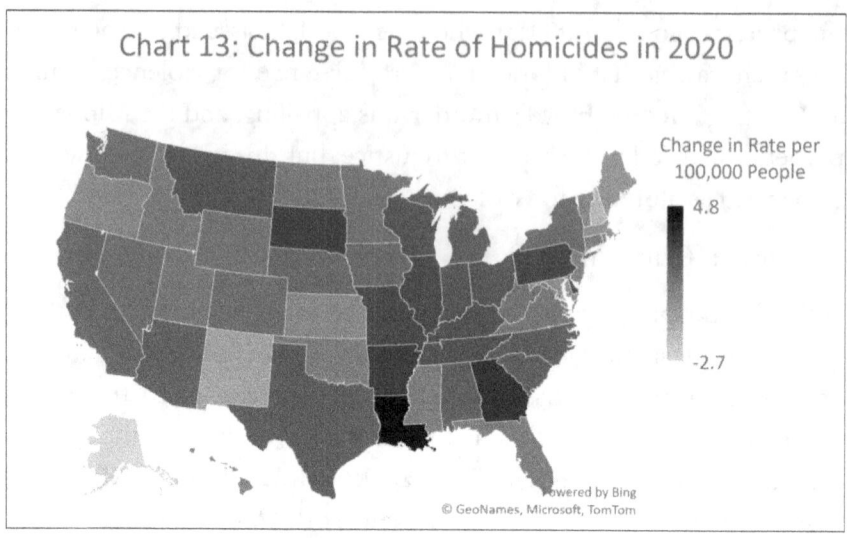

Source: FBI Crime Data Explorer.[60]

Florida experienced a much larger decline in the rate of property crime in 2020 at 375.4 per 100,000 people than the other mega-states. California only decreased 196.9 and Texas 160.6, and New York increased 24.6.

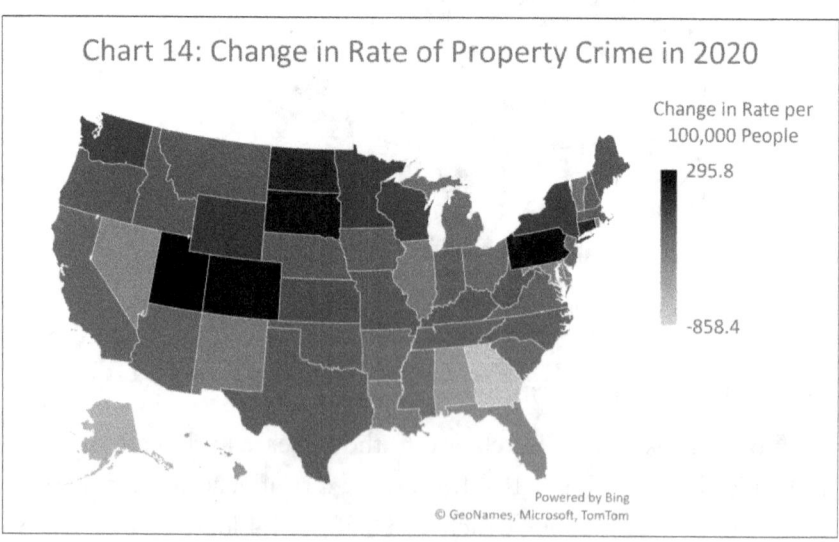

Source: FBI Crime Data Explorer.[61]

More Crime in 2021 Too

In 2021, there was an outbreak of murders in many large American cities but not in Miami where murders were down 15.5 per cent.[62] Sixteen cities set recent records for the number of homicides. These cities included: Albuquerque, New Mexico; Atlanta, Georgia; Austin, Texas; Baton Rouge, Louisiana; Columbus, Ohio; Indianapolis, Indiana; Jackson, Mississippi; Louisville, Kentucky; Macon, Georgia; Milwaukee, Wisconsin; New Haven, Connecticut; Philadelphia, Pennsylvania; Portland, Oregon; Rochester, New York; St. Paul, Minnesota; and Tucson, Arizona.[63] It was no coincidence that twelve of these cities were run by Democrat administrations. Many of them had experienced protests following the George Floyd killing and had imprudently cut police budgets in response to the defund the police movement.

The step-up in murders in 2021 was confirmed by data shared by an FBI analyst with the *New York Times*. It showed a murder rate of 6.5 per 100,00, which was the highest since 1969. The rates were the highest in many years in Chicago, New York, Los Angeles, and Minneapolis to name a few of the largest cities.[64]

In contrast, in Florida Governor DeSantis and other members of his Cabinet strongly supported the police. On October 25, 2021, the Governor announced his intention to offer a $5,000 relocation bonus to attract disaffected police from cities like New York, Minneapolis, and Seattle that had cut police budgets and didn't have their backs. He was seeking to take advantage of the imposition of vaccine mandates that was viewed by many officers as the last straw. The bonus was offered to help the state's police and sheriff's departments to recruit experienced law enforcement professionals and to make them feel welcome.[65]

The Florida legislature also passed an anti-riot bill in April 2021 that was signed into law by Governor DeSantis. It increased penalties for crimes committed during a riot and created new felonies for being involved in violent demonstrations. It also authorized the detention of offenders until their court appearances. In September, a Federal judge in Tallahassee ruled that the new law was unconstitutional on First Amendment grounds., but this ruling is under appeal.[66]

California voters approved Proposition 47 in 2014. Among other things, it recategorized from felonies to misdemeanors various property crimes under a $950 threshold as well as personal drug use.[67] While it took several years for criminals to seize the opportunities, Proposition 47 along with relaxed bail and the election of liberal soft-on-crime prosecutors, most notably Chesa Boudin in San Francisco and George Gascon in Los Angeles, led to the outbreak of "smash and grab" robberies that have become nightly fare on Fox News.

Floridians needn't worry, however. The Attorney General Ashley Moody has reassured them that she and the Governor are taking steps to ensure that Florida "doesn't become California or Minnesota." These include a database of repeat offenders who will be targeted for prosecution.[68]

Even in the Golden State people are getting fed-up with out-of-control crime. An indication that the tide may be starting to turn in a city plagued by robberies and aberrant street behavior of druggies and the homeless is the crude announcement by San Francisco Mayor London Breed of a "crackdown" on "the bullshit that has destroyed our city."[69]

6
PEOPLE KEEP COMING

From April 1, 2020, two weeks after Governor DeSantis issued the executive order locking down the state until July 1, 2021, when the census was taken, the population of Florida grew by 242,941 or 1.1 percent. This continuation of Florida's strong population growth occurred while the country was only experiencing meager growth of 444,464 or 0.1 per cent because of "decreased net international migration, decreased fertility, and increased mortality due in part to the COVID-19 pandemic," according to the United States Census Bureau.[70]

The Florida Legislature's Office of Economic & Demographic Research expects this population boom to continue unabated averaging 309,867 net new residents per year between April 1, 2021, and April 1, 2026, and recording an average annual growth rate of 1.41 percent. This amounts to an average increase in population of 849 people per day over the five-year period.[71]

The population increase in Florida from April 1, 2020, to July 1, 2021, reported by the Bureau of the Census resulted mainly from the net in-migration from other states of 263,958 or 579 people per day over the fifteen-month period.

The Florida Department of Highway Safety and Motor Vehicles' records show that between September 2020 and March 2021, 33,565

New York driver's licenses were swapped for Florida ones. And that, over the more-than two-year period from 2019 to April 2021, 104,960 came from New York, followed by 53,901 from New Jersey, 48,143 from Georgia, 46,042 from Illinois, and 43,801 from California, all of which except for neighboring Georgia were blue states.[72]

The Florida population increase was also bolstered by the net arrival of 41,260 immigrants from abroad. Total net migration was thus 305,218. This net migration more than offset the natural decrease in the population resulting from deaths exceeding births by a margin of 58,203 over this period.

Most other states did not record robust population growth like Florida (Chart 15). New York declined by 365,336, the most of any state, and California was next in line with a decrease of 300,387, followed by Illinois which dropped by 141,039. The common features of these three states depressing their population levels are their tight Covid restrictions, increases in murder rates, and high taxes, all of which have resulted from policies pursued by their Democratic state governments. In contrast, Republican Texas exhibited an even larger population increase than Florida at 382,436.

The red state-blue state divergence in population growth is a country-wide phenomenon. States classified as Republican in 2020 by Ballotpedia.org registered a population increase of 1,195,085 over the April 1, 2020, to July 1, 2021, period, states classified as Democrat recorded a population decrease of 711,353, and, in states where Republicans and Democrats shared power, the population went down 39,268.[73]

FLORIDA DREAMS LIVE ON THROUGH COVID-19

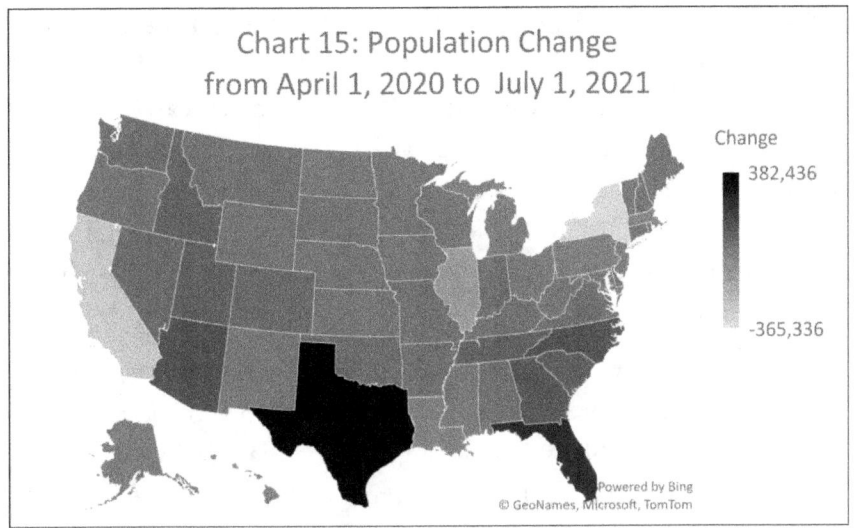

Source: U.S. Census Bureau.[74]

Blue State Residents Chaffing under Tighter Covid Restrictions

During the period since the onset of Covid (for which data is available), Florida had a net inflow of 263,958 residents of other states (including the District of Columbia and Puerto Rico) taking up residence in Florida. This is net of the Florida residents who moved to other states. It made Florida the state receiving the largest net domestic migration (Chart 16). The only state that came close to this large of net in-migration was the fellow red mega-state of Texas with 211,289. In contrast, the states experiencing the largest net loss of residents were the blue states of California with 429,383, New York with 406,257, and Illinois with 151,512. While the Census Bureau hasn't yet broken down the recent source of in-migrants to Florida by state of origin, in the final decades of the Twentieth Century, New York was the largest source of in-migrants, and Illinois and California were also important sources.[75] And even though it's impossible to say exactly why each in-migrant moved to Florida, the sunny warm climate couldn't have hurt, but higher taxes and Covid restrictions no doubt must have also played a role. People sometimes vote with their feet.

These migration trends were confirmed by the U-Haul Growth Index, which is calculated as the "net gain of one-way U-Haul trucks entering a state versus leaving that state in a calendar year." According to the recently released data on one-way, do-it-yourself movers for 2021, Florida was barely edged out of the number one position by Texas. And blue New York and California were at the bottom of the list with California ranked dead last because of all the people moving out.[76]

One of the New York City residents moving was Karol Markowicz, a reporter who was raised in Brooklyn and had three kids born in Manhattan. She said that she loved her native city and never imagined she would go to live anywhere else. Yet she moved to Florida. The dealbreaker for her was how New York so readily caved to the teacher's union and shut down her children's' schools and then, when the schools finally reopened, made all the children wear masks.[77] Judging from the outward flow of people, there must be others with similar motives for their move. Florida has become a shining city on a hill for many Northerners, like America was for many early settlers, just by staying open and remaining normal.

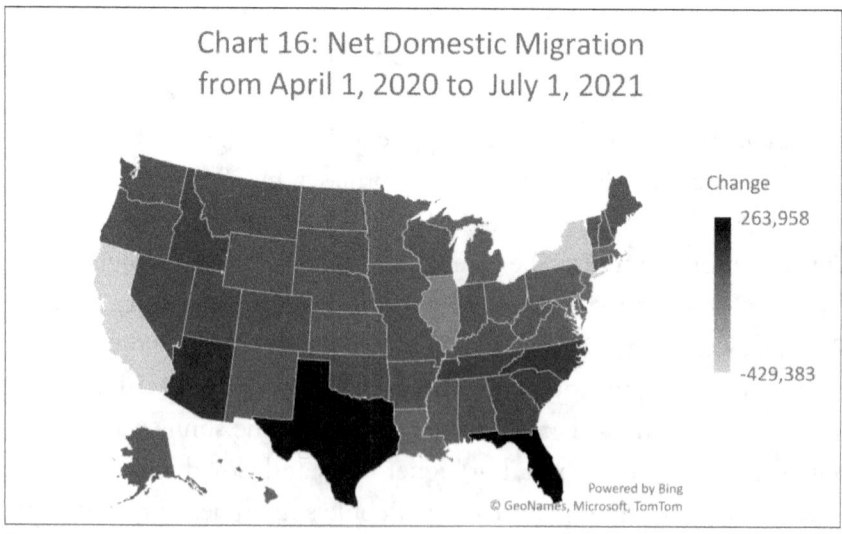

Source: U.S. Census Bureau.[78]

Immigrants Seeking Opportunities

Florida is not only the state with the largest net domestic migration, but also the state with the highest net international immigration since Covid hit (Chart 17). It received 41,260 net international immigrants. This may seem like a small number, but it is a large share of the 256,869 total net international immigrants over the period recorded for the whole country by the Census Bureau. This total evidently does not take into account the unprecedentedly large flows of illegal immigrants since January 2021 when Joe Biden became president and opened the southern border to massive inflows.[79] Thus these numbers must be taken with a larger grain of salt than usual. Nevertheless, for what it's worth, the number of net international immigrants welcomed by Florida reported by the Census Department was much higher than received by Texas (28,503), California (13,861), New York (18,860), all of which are also mega-states that traditionally receive large numbers of international immigrants.

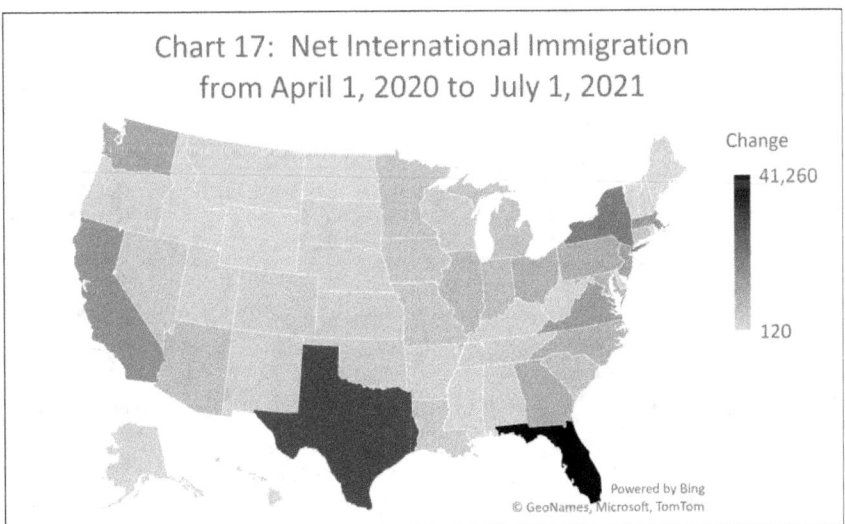

Source: U.S. Census Bureau.[80]

While Governor DeSantis supports legal immigration, he has been extremely critical of the Biden Administration's colossal failure to enforce border laws. In response to news of the Federal Government's clandestine flights without warning in the middle of the night to dump illegal immigrants in Florida and other states across the country, DeSantis raised the possibility of bussing the illegals up to President Biden's home state of Delaware. It may have been a tongue in cheek remark, but it reflected Governor DeSantis's profound opposition to the Administration's open border policies.[81]

7
PROTESTING THE CRACKDOWN IN CUBA

After Fidel Castro took power in Cuba in 1959 and imposed a harsh communist police state on the erstwhile jewel of the Caribbean, a half a million Cubans, including large numbers of the country's professional and business elite, fled to Miami seeking refuge. Over the years, they multiplied to over a million and a half people of Cuban ethnicity living in Florida, mostly in Miami-Dade. It wasn't long before they became Cuban Americans and contributed much to the development of Florida and became the dominant force in the politics and culture of Miami. Because of their visceral opposition to communism, they voted overwhelmingly Republican and staunchly opposed regularization of relations with Cuba, hoping in vain that U.S. sanctions would eventually lead to the fall of communism in their former country. However, as the memories of the brutal treatment that they and their families received at the hands of the savage communist regime faded, younger generations became less steadfast in their opposition to the Cuban government and the solid Republican Cuban American voting block began to crumble.

Cuban Protests Spread to Miami and Beyond

In early spring 2021, hope for the reestablishment of democracy in Cuba was rekindled when Raúl Castro stepped down as First Secretary of the Party and was succeeded by Miguel Dias-Canel, who had replaced Castro as president two years earlier. This ended over

60-year iron-fisted domination of Cuba by the Castro brothers. However, plus ça change.

In the sweltering July heat in a country where dissent had been squelched for six decades and the flame of democracy extinguished, anti-government protests, which had been simmering below the radar screen, burst out in Havana, led by brave young dissidents, and spread across Cuba. Superficially, the complaints were over food and fuel shortages, and other economic woes, but the underlying fundamental demand was for freedom. Like wildfire, it didn't take long before these protests sparked demonstrations in Miami, Tampa, and elsewhere in Florida where there were concentrations of Cuban Americans longing to see their former country free. Massive demonstrations supporting the Cuban dissidents were held at Miami's Freedom Tower and outside the Versailles Restaurant, an iconic eatery at the heart of Miami's Little Havana. It was here that Yotuel Romero, and a group of other Cuban rappers sang *Patria y Vida*, which became the unofficial anthem of the protestors.[82] Its title is a play on the omnipresent Cuban Communist revolutionary slogan *Patria o Muerte*. It means that the Cuban people want their country and their life, not death which was all the Communist Government had to offer.[83] The popularity of the song indicates that the younger generation of Cubans has woke up to the yearning of the Cuban people for freedom and democracy and has finally become attached to the cause emotionally. The Miami demonstrations featured a who's who of Florida Republican politicians including Governor DeSantis and Senator Marco Rubio, a Cuban American himself, and even a few Democrats.

Demonstrations resumed in Miami on November 14 to support the "Civic March for Change" planned for the same day in Havana. The march was in support of human and civil rights and of the more than a thousand people who had been detained, and of the hundreds still being held in jail following the July 15 protests. While it was repressed by the Cuban Government as usual and fizzled, demonstrators still marched in Miami in support.[84]

A group on Facebook called Archipiélago with thirty-eight thousand members provides important support to the dissident community in Cuba. It helps to coordinate some of the demonstrations.[85]

When Cubans again becomes free as they inevitably must, it will be with the whole-hearted support of Florida's Cuban Americans. While they were forced to leave their homeland by a brutal dictatorship, they became Americans and Floridians by choice. Yet they never forgot their relatives back in Cuba suffering under the boot of Communist tyranny.

Consequences for the Ballot Box

At the end of 2014, having won his second term with the support of Florida voters, including almost half of Miami-Dade's Cuban American community, President Barack Obama, whose heart always leaned left, made the calculation that he could reverse the U.S. Government's hardline policies against the Communist government in Cuba at a low political cost. Consequently, President Obama declared that "he was rejecting the failed, Cold War-era policy era of the past to chart a new course in Cuba." In the months that followed his Administration did just this and moved to normalize relations with Cuba. The following July his Administration reopened the U.S. Embassy in Havana. While he could not lift the trade embargo without Congressional approval, he took the steps he could using executive actions and tried to make the changes "irreversible." Regulations were eased and trade and travel restrictions were curtailed. In March 2016, President Obama became the first president in 88 years to visit Cuba. Older Cuban Americans gagged on seeing the pictures of Cuban President Raúl Castro awkwardly holding up President Obama's arm in triumph,[86] but polls suggested that younger Cuban Americans didn't care much.[87] It was probably this softening of Cuban American opinion towards Cuba that emboldened President Obama to embark on his "new course" in the first place. Policy often follows the polls.

Opinions subsequently hardened in the Cuban American community when Cuba failed to become more democratic. This enabled Donald Trump in 2016 to get 54 percent of the Cuban American vote, which helped to put Florida's 29 electoral votes in his column. Subsequently in June 2017, expressing concern over human rights abuses and mistrust of the "brutal" Communist Government, President Trump reimposed many of the trade, travel, and fund transmittal restrictions on Cuba, but did not go so far as to close the Embassy or cancel commercial flights.[88] For good measure, though, on his way out the White House door in January 2021, President Trump reinstated the designation of Cuba as a "state sponsor of terrorism" with all the additional sanctions that that carries.[89]

The protests in the summer of 2021 widened the cleavage between the Biden Administration and Cuban Americans. Many were disappointed with the lukewarm response of the Administration to the protests and the failure to take any concrete supporting action such as restoring the protestors' access to the internet as was demanded by Governor DeSantis. Black Lives Matter, an important force on the Democrat progressive left, couldn't have chosen a worse time to make its call for an end of the trade embargo, right in the middle of the protests, and without so much as a word about the Cuban Government's repression of dissent and violation of human rights.[90]

The fallout from the Cuban anti-government protests is certainly not favorable for the Biden Administration. It will only be able to return to Obama-era policies towards Cuba at a substantial cost in terms of lost Cuban American votes. A new poll released in March before the protests shows 66 percent opposed. And Republican support seems to be growing. Donald Trump won 62 percent of the Cuban American vote in 2020, up 8-percentage-points from 2016 and holding at that level even after losing the election.[91]

8
THE ECONOMY REBOUNDS STRONGLY

Like for all state economies, real GDP (in millions of chained 2012 dollars) in Florida declined precipitously from the first quarter of 2020 to the second quarter as non-essential activities in the national and state economies were shuttered because of Covid (Chart 18). The fall in Florida real GDP at 8.9 percent was virtually identical to the average decline in national GDP. California and Texas decreased by slightly more, but the difference was only in tenths of a percentage point. New York fell by about 1 ¾ percent less.

And, like all other states, the Florida economy was cushioned by the large increases in personal income resulting from Federal transfer payments providing income support (Chart 19). This reached a maximum of over 15 percent of income in the first quarter of 2021 when payments from two separate Federal stimulus programs were made at around the same time. The support dropped in the second and third quarter of 2021, but personal income remained about 10 percent above pre-Covid levels.

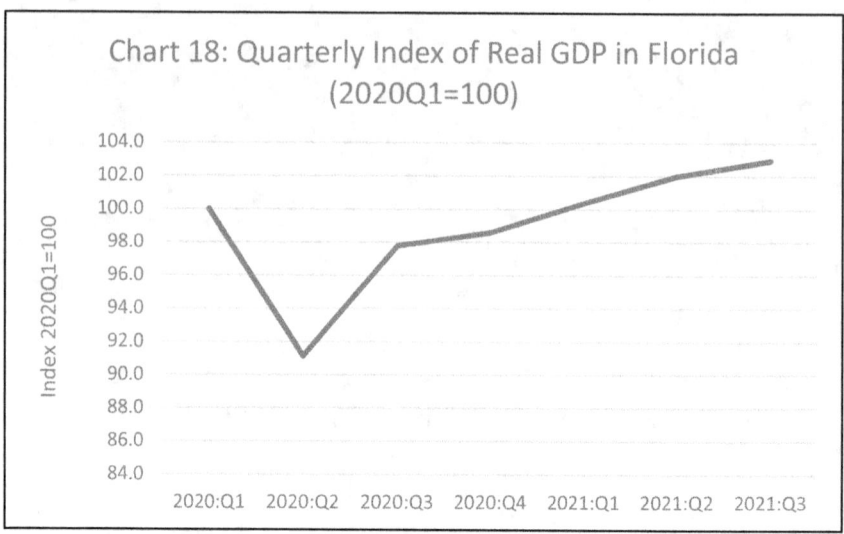

Source: Bureau of Economic Analysis, Regional Data.[92]

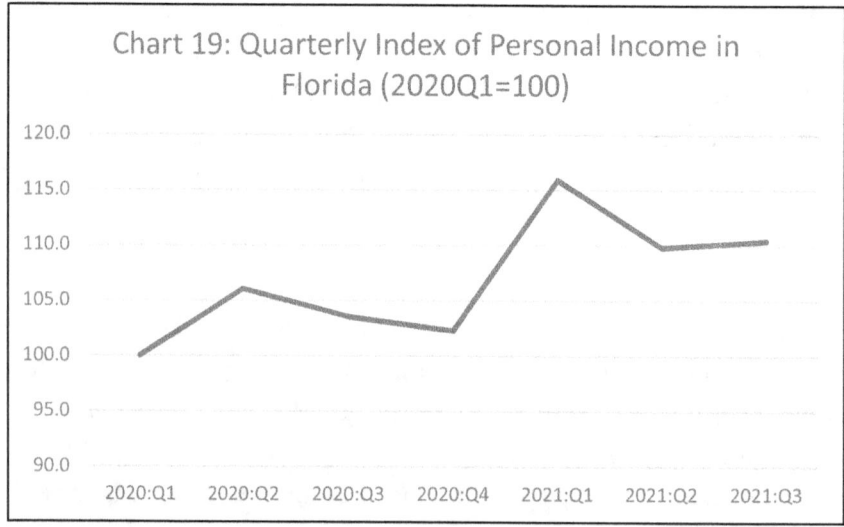

Source: Bureau of Economic Analysis, Regional Data.[93]

While Not as Much as in New York and California

Once the Florida economy was unleashed at the end of April and boosted by the same unprecedented dose of fiscal and monetary stimulus that kept the national economy afloat, the economy bounced back strongly.[94] By early 2021, it had surpassed its pre-Covid level and by the third quarter of 2021, it was up by about 3 percent, which was less than two tenth of a percent higher than the increase in the national economy over the same period. However, this left its recovery significantly weaker than the 4.9 percent recovery experienced in New York, and behind the 3.6 percent recorded in California. Florida was in the middle of the pack as far as its recovery in GDP was concerned and only a little above Texas which increased 2.8 per cent. (Chart 20).

Source: Bureau of Economic Analysis, Regional Data.[95]

The slow recovery of Florida compared to California and New York, states that were locked down more tightly may seem counterintuitive, but there is a good explanation. The composition of output in these two states made them less subject to Covid-related disruptions (Table 1). The key difference is the much larger share of information in California and New York, and of finance and insurance in New York. California is home to Silicon Valley and Hollywood and New York is the nation's financial capital. And Democratic Washington is the headquarters of Amazon, which gobbled up a lot of business from people stuck home during Covid. These industries were better able to continue to operate and even have their employees work remotely from home. They were thus able still to grow robustly right despite Covid. In contrast, Florida is more dependent than these other states on tourism, an industry that requires the face-to-face delivery of services and that was depressed by Covid fears and restrictions. Texas, the other mega-state, grew almost as fast as Florida based on the growth of its relatively large manufacturing sector, which expanded enough to offset the downward pull of decreased output from oil and gas extraction.

Table 1: Comparison of Key Differences in Sectoral Composition of Real GDP						
	Mining, Quarrying, and Oil & Gas Extraction	Manu-facturing	Infor-mation	Finance and Insurance	Arts, Entertainment and Recreation	Accomo-dation and Food Services
National Growth of Industry 20Q1 to 21Q3 (Percent)	-17.6	4.2	16.2	15.5	-12.1	2.7
Percentage Share of Economy in 20Q3						
Total US	2.1	11.9	7.6	7.1	0.8	2.5
Florida	0.1	5.6	5.7	6.2	1.3	3.9
California	0.5	13.2	14.5	4.7	1.1	2.1
New York	0.1	4.6	12.7	17.8	1.2	2.1
Texas	11.2	12.9	4.6	5.2	0.5	2.2

Source: Bureau of Economic Analysis, Regional Data.

Reopening Spurred Better Job Growth

Florida's heavy reliance on tourism and the delivery of in-person services made it more difficult and costly to lock down and subsequently restrict much of the private service sector of the economy for very long. That is an important reason Governor DeSantis pivoted Florida so early compared to the large Democratic states from concentrating exclusively on containing Covid to allowing Floridians to get back to work and get on with their lives as soon as it became apparent that it was reasonably safe to do so.

The success of this strategy is evident in the strong rebound in total nonfarm employment in Florida (Chart 21). After falling 14 percent from February to April 2020 over the course of the initial lockdown, Florida regained almost all the lost ground by December 2022, by which time employment was only down 1.1 percent from

February levels.

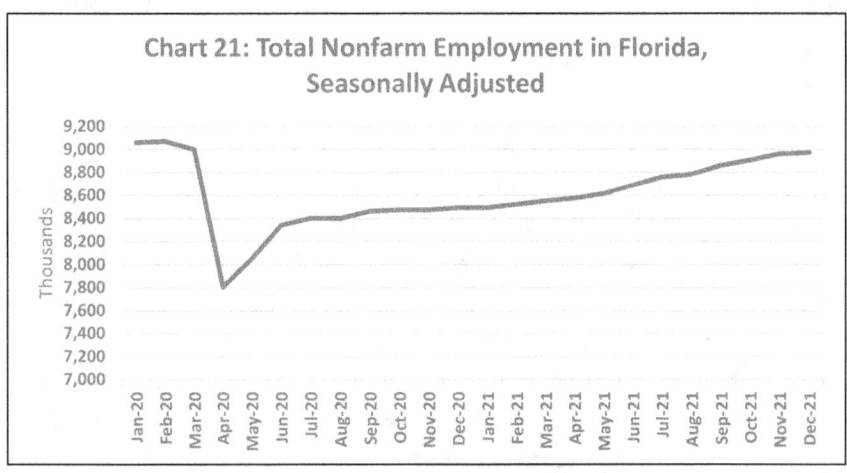

Source: Bureau of Labor Statistics. Key Economic Indicators in a Time of Covid.[96]

The recovery in employment in Florida up to November 2021 was stronger than in most states (Chart 22). In fact, Florida had the 10th strongest recovery among the fifty states and the District of Columbia. Not a single Democratic state had a better performance. And the employment level in Florida was significantly better than the average for the United States, which was still down 2.3 percent by December 2021. Moreover, in relation to the other Mega-states, Florida's performance was even more impressive. In December 2021 employment in New York was still down by 8.1 percent from February 2020 levels and California was down 4.6 per cent. The difference between the real GDP performance of these states and their employment growth is striking. This is an indication that all residents of these states are not participating in the recovery, and that its fruits are being concentrated in higher wage industries like tech and finance that have been able to benefit from Covid. This will tend to increase inequality and disadvantage the groups, including minorities, which are more likely to be unemployed.

Texas is the only Mega-state that had a better employment performance than Florida, already being up by 0.7 percent in employment by December 2021. And it is not a coincidence that it is also a state with a Republican as Governor and in charge in both the state senate and house and with less restrictive policies to deal with Covid (as measured by a relatively low Oxford Stringency Index in 2021).

If the states are ranked in terms of the strength of their employment recovery by December 2021, the first Democratic state is Colorado, which is ranked 15th. The lower on the list, the more Democratic states are found. The state with the largest shortfall of employment in December 2021 is Hawaii, another Democratic state, which has by far the strictest Covid restrictions of all the states according to the Oxford Stringency Index. It has an even smaller manufacturing, information, and finance and insurance sectors than Florida and an even larger accommodation and food services industry, which would make it even more vulnerable than Florida to job losses resulting from Covid restrictions. Its experience should serve as an object lesson on how harmful excessive restrictions can be to states reliant on face-to-face delivered service industries.

On average by December 2022, employment in Democrat run states was down 4.7 percent from February 2020 levels, whereas employment in Republican states was only down 1.3 percent. Employment in states with divided party governments were down by 4.1 percent, again much more than in Republican governed states.

The Unemployment Rate Spiked, then Dropped Back

The unemployment rose sharply after the Florida economy was shut down in March/April 2020, rising from an unusually low level of 3.3 percent in February to 14.2 percent in May (Chart 23). After the economy was reopened it steadily dropped to 4.4 per cent in December 2021. While this is still above its pre-Covid levels, it represents a very tight labor market where many employers are having trouble finding willing workers.

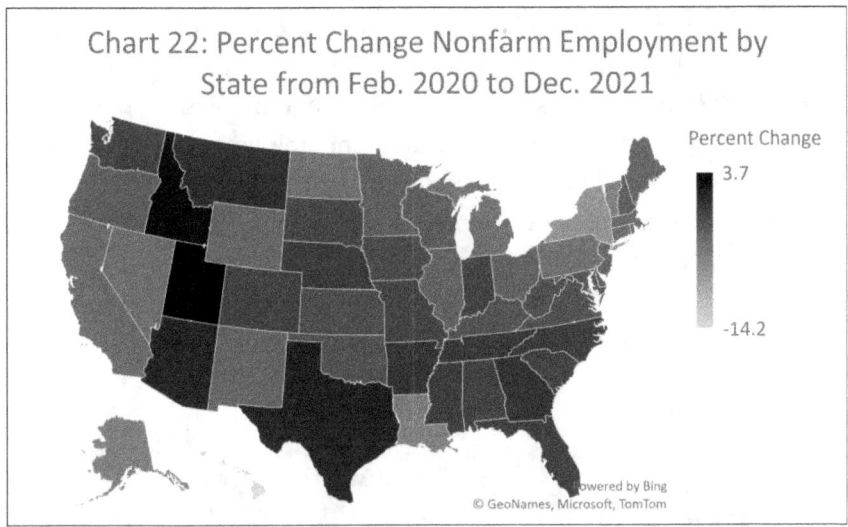

Source: Bureau of Labor Statistics, Key Economic Indicators in a Time of Covid.[97]

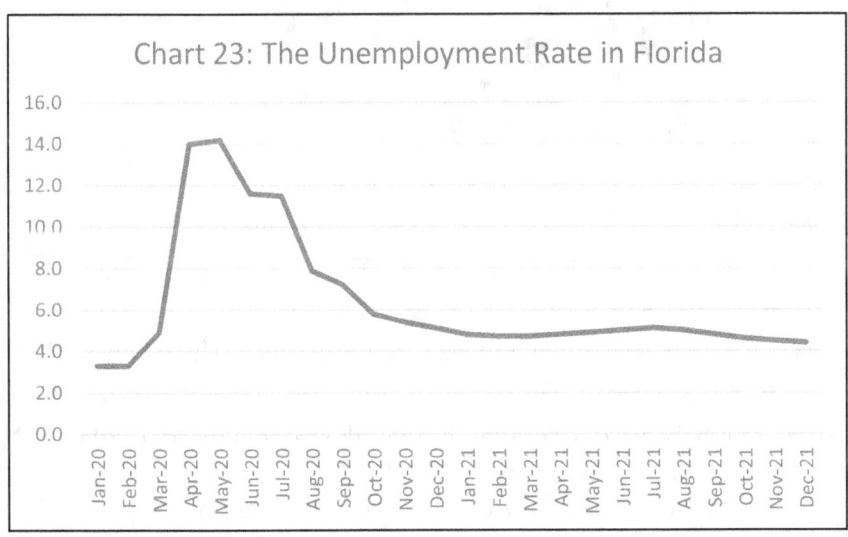

Source: Bureau of Labor Statistics.[98]

While Florida's unemployment rate is low, it is not as low as many other states (Chart 24). In fact, Florida's unemployment at 4.4 percent in December 2021 put it in 27th place in the middle of the pack. However, it was much lower than the 6.5 percent recorded in California and 6.2 percent in New York, the two Mega-states with the most Covid restrictions. Florida's rate was also lower than Texas's 5.0

percent. There is a pattern here that reflects the stringency of Covid policies as influenced by the politics of the different states. By December 2021, the red states had average unemployment rates of 3.2 percent whereas the blue states had unemployment rates of 5.3 percent, more than 2 percentage points higher. Democrat California was the state with the highest unemployment of 6.5 percent and Republican Nebraska had the lowest at 1.7 percent.

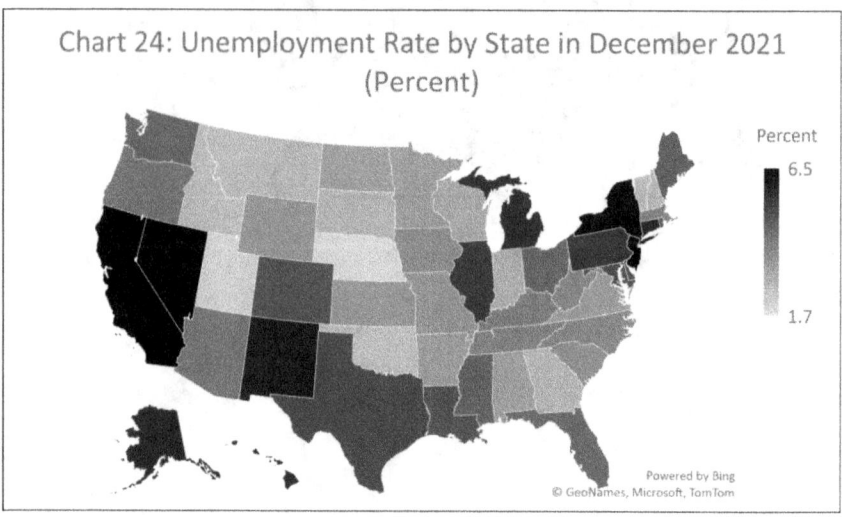

Source: Bureau of Labor Statistics.[99]

There is much evidence that unemployment not only results in lost earnings during the time of joblessness, but that it adversely affects future employment and earnings prospects.[100] This might also apply to those who drop out of the labor force because of fears of Covid, but who are not counted as unemployed. This phenomenon is called "scarring" and is particularly damaging to young people entering the labor force whose whole work lives may be impaired. In addition, there are serious social impacts of unemployment. According to a survey of the literature, these include "mental illness, social isolation, crime, and suicide."[101] Florida's policy of keeping the economy open during Covid probably served to mitigate these effects compared the states like New York and California that implemented more restrictive policies that raised unemployment.

Federal Policy Created Voluntary Unemployment

At the end of March 2020, the Federal Government introduced the Coronavirus Aid, Relief, and Economic Security (CARES) Act, which was the first of several measures expanding unemployment insurance to provide income support to those furloughed by the shutdown of their employers to curtail Covid. Initially, it paid for the states to extend unemployment insurance for beneficiaries by an additional 13 weeks. It also paid $600 per week in Pandemic Unemployment Compensation (PUC) on top of state benefits. This payment gave many people more money from staying home from unemployment insurance than they could have ever been able to earn on the job.[102] The $600 top-up was allowed to expire at the end of July 2020. But it was replaced by a less generous $300 payment that was authorized in December and extended to September 6, 2021.[103] This was still a large work disincentive but smaller.

It's very difficult to deny benefits offered by the Federal Government to a state's citizens even if they are likely to have negative effects on the state's economy. Thus, Florida fell into the same unemployment trap as did the other states. The Covid-related increases in unemployment insurance were roundly criticized by employers who found it increasingly difficult to get workers. The problem of labor shortages was much greater in Florida than in the other Mega-states that aren't as heavily reliant on lower-wage service sector jobs where attachment to particular employers is not as strong. It is in comparison to these less remunerative jobs that the higher unemployment insurance looks most attractive.

At Governor DeSantis's behest, Florida terminated the enhanced unemployment insurance benefits early, on June 26, 2021. The reason given was that there were "almost half a million job openings in the state of Florida." At the same time, the Governor announced that "the work search requirement [which had been suspended due to Covid] will return for those receiving unemployment benefits."[104] These steps gave Florida a two-month head start in returning to a more normal labor market without the Covid-related work disincentives. In addition, the duration and level of benefits in Florida is low as befits Florida's lower wage level.

In January 2022, Florida offered 12 weeks of unemployment insurance benefits, which tied it with North Carolina for the fewest weeks available among all of the states. The Mega-states of California, New York, and Texas all offered 26 weeks of benefits (Chart 25).

The reduced role of unemployment insurance in Florida and the other Republican States compared to the Democratic states is evident in the different average duration of unemployment insurance in red states, and blue states, which is 23.8 weeks, and 27.6 weeks, respectively, a difference of 3.7 weeks. And the only states still with extended benefit durations after the Federal Government withdrew financing are New Mexico, and New Jersey, again both Democratic states.

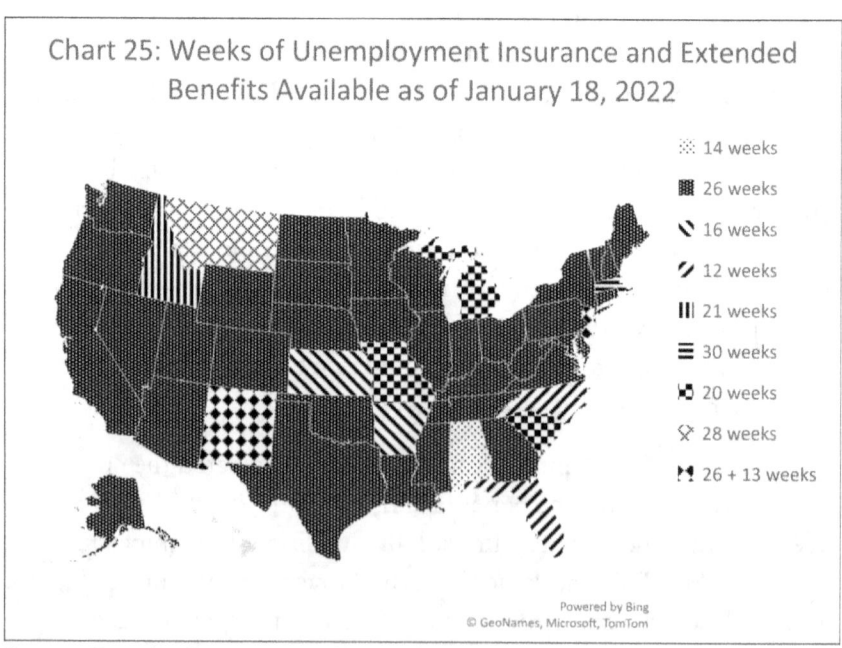

Source: Source: Center on Budget and Policy Priorities, "Policy Basics: How Many Weeks of Unemployment Compensation Are Available?" Updated January 18, 2022.[105]

Florida Finances Are Still Strong

At the outset of Covid, there was concern that state government finances would deteriorate so much that they would face a budgetary crisis. A stream of Federal Acts was passed to deal with the pandemic and to provide support to counter its depressing effect on the economy. The first was the Coronavirus Aid, Relief and Economic Security Act (CARES), which was signed into law by President Trump on March 27, 2020, and contained $2.2 trillion in funding. Then came the Coronavirus Response and Relief Supplemental Appropriation Act 2021 (CRRSA), which was penned by President Trump on December 27, 2000, at the end of his term and contained $900 billion in stimulus. Next came the American Rescue Plan Act of 2021 (ARPA) which was the Biden Administration's $1.9 trillion contribution to Covid relief signed on March 11, 2021. These acts, which together constituted the largest stimulus package in American history, not only fattened the bank accounts of Americans and their businesses, but also bolstered the coffers of state governments.

With all this money available, it should not be surprising that the fiscal position of the Government of the State of Florida strengthened during Covid, rather than deteriorating as was feared.[106] In the fiscal year 2021-2022, which runs from July 1, 2021, to June 30, 2022, the Florida Government is budgeting for $101.5 billion in spending. This represents a $9.2-billion increase over the prior fiscal year. Of this increase, $6.9 billion, or three-quarters, comes from the Federal Government, most of which is for Covid relief.[107]

The growth of general revenues, including sales tax, which accounts for over three quarters of Florida revenues, has been less than expected because of the impact of Covid on the economy, especially the decline of tourism. However, revenues have been making up the gap as the economy strengthens.

In addition, Florida had per-capita debt of only $1,313 in 2021, making it the 5th lowest of the states in that year.[108] This combined with the strength of Florida's revenues have earned it a triple A credit rating from all three major credit rating agencies, putting it in a good position to finance its continued growth even after the special Federal Covid transfers cease. In contrast, many other states like New York, New Jersey, Illinois and even California, which have lower credit ratings, will suffer a fiscal hangover when these payments are cut off.[109]

9
A MAGNET FOR COMPANIES

Companies, Big and Small, Come to Florida

Since the onset of Covid, companies galore have moved to Florida, not necessarily their head offices but major operations. They come for the low-tax, business friendly climate, but Covid restrictions elsewhere also played a role. They are in many industries including the financial services, entertainment, and even food services. This chapter presents some of the most notable that have been in the press.

The movement of financial firms to Palm Beach, Broward, and Miami-Dade counties in Southeast Florida has been a favorite theme. There is ample anecdotal evidence that this continued during Covid and maybe even accelerated. The senior executives and investors in the financial service industry, who holed up in Florida with their families during the height of Covid when Manhattan was a ghost town, discovered that, thanks to modern information technology, they could do their work remotely just as easily in Florida as they could in New York. Some of them liked living in Florida so much that they didn't want to go back. And if they were important enough in their companies, they were able to do this and bring parts or even the whole of their businesses down with them.

Financial service behemoth Goldman Sachs, which has become synonymous with Wall Street and all that metonym connotes, announced its plans to move part of its asset management division to Palm Beach where the folks have tons of assets to manage. A hundred employees including partners will be making the move.[110] But this may just be the opening gambit.

Hedge fund Elliott Management with assets of $41 billion is in the process leasing office space for its headquarters in West Palm Beach.[111]

Carl Icahn, a billionaire born and bred in New York City, officially completed the move of his company Icahn Enterprises out of his hometown to Sunny Isles Beach in Miami-Dade County.[112] Icahn Enterprises LP is "a diversified holding company with subsidiaries engaged in the following operating businesses: Investment, Energy, Automotive, Food Packaging, Metals, Real Estate, Home Fashion and… Pharma." It has assets of $25 billion and is 92 percent owned by Icahn.[113]

Investment powerhouse Blackstone, with $619 billion under management,[114] plans to open an office in Miami.[115] In January 2021, it leased 41,000 square feet to house its tech staff at 2 MiamiCentral near Brightline's main railroad station. Later in March, it bought this building and its sister at 3 MiamiCentral for $230 million.[116] This will give it plenty of room for expansion.

The Miami mayor Francis Suarez is a big enthusiast of cryptocurrencies like Bitcoin. These are digital encrypted pseudo currencies that are maintained by blockchain technology and that are believed by some to be a way of transferring the currency issuing function of the government into private hands. Mayor Suarez has been working tirelessly to turn Miami into an industry center with conferences and even took his salary in Bitcoin. Whether this will turn out to be a wise strategy, of course, very much remains to be seen. The industry's volatility and risk exposure due to the questionable legal status of some of the activities it facilitates, which, needless to say, are frowned on by governments and central banks.

Suarez's greatest success was getting Blockchain.com, a large financial service company specializing in crypto currencies, to move its U.S. headquarters to Miami from New York.[117] Blockchain operates a major cryptocurrency exchange and wallet as well as data and analytical products for investors, which makes it a major player in the arcane world of cryptocurrencies. This company was valued at $5.2 billion in 2021 following a round of investment offerings that brought in $300 million.[118] Suarez has also attracted other cryptocurrency firms to set up or expand in Miami, including MoonPay, Orca Capital, FTX US, eToro, and Bit Digital.[119]

The Walt Disney Company is the largest Florida company not officially headquartered in Florida with 77,000 employees at Disney World near Orlando where, like a medieval baron, it lords over 48 square miles, giving it lots of room to grow.[120] In July 2021, it announced that it was planning on moving 2,000 jobs from Burbank, California over the next 18 months to the Lake Nona community where it had purchased 60 acres to build a new regional campus. The employees will be mostly from the Parks, Experiences and Products division. Walt Disney Imagineering, the creative arm of The Walt Disney Company, is also expected to move.[121] This move has fueled speculation about bigger things to come.[122]

Lake Nona has also attracted the KPMG Lakehouse, which is the Big Four accounting firm's $430 million global training and innovation center with rooms for eight hundred people.[123]

Carrier Global, the air-conditioning manufacturer, which had been spun off by United Technologies Corporation, announced in March 2020 that it was moving its headquarters to Palm Beach Gardens.[124] While this had nothing to do with Covid, it was the largest company recently to move its headquarters to Florida. Even ignoring the favorable business climate, where better than Florida to locate a company that makes air conditioners? It would make proud John Gorrie, the Apalachicola doctor who Floridians consider the inventor of air-conditioning.[125]

During the early days of Covid in May 2020, Elon Musk's Tesla auto plant was still shut down in Fremont, California by overbearing county health regulations, while other automobile manufacturers in other states were still cranking out cars. After publicly voicing his dissatisfaction with the local authorities, he got away with opening the factory in defiance of their dictates.[126] But that wasn't the end of the story. At Tesla's annual meeting in October 2021, Musk announced his intention to move himself and his headquarters to Texas. And it wasn't long, December 1, 2021, to be precise, before a press release and SEC filing announced the move of Tesla's corporate headquarters from Palo Alto, California to Austin, Texas.[127] Too bad he didn't choose Florida, but California was still the big loser.

The restaurant industry was one of the hardest hit by Covid. After being shut down for a prolonged period, it was only allowed to open begrudgingly, with outside seating and limited capacity constraints that made it difficult, if not impossible, to make ends meet. In comparison, the restrictions in Florida were short lived and offered opportunities for restauranteurs with cash still in their pockets. The lockdown was a factor in encouraging the New York based Major Food Group to diversify its holdings by moving into South Florida. They have already opened several restaurants in Miami and have plans for more elsewhere in the state.[128] The lockdown also pushed other New York restaurants to set up in The Oasis in Wynwood in Miami.[129] The Oasis is a trendy new development that is being anchored by the Latin American headquarters of Spotify, a music streaming service that is also a new Florida arrival.

At the lower end of the food service industry, Subway, the ubiquitous submarine sandwich seller, announced that in early 2022 it is going to move its "'consumer facing' businesses to Miami, including culinary, marketing and 'global transformation.'" This came on the heels of a lay-off of five hundred employees in its Milford, Connecticut headquarters earlier last year due to Covid-related losses in sales.[130] Again this could be the beginning of something bigger.[131]

There are many other smaller, less known examples throughout the state too numerous to mention. For instance, in August 2020, Civix, a leading company providing software to the public sector, opened in a center of excellence in Heathrow, Florida,[132] and, in the summer of 2021, Sonesta International Hotels established a new corporate office in downtown Orlando overlooking Lake Eola.[133] You get the picture. Florida was attractive before Covid with its low taxes and business friendly climate. Covid just made it more so.

Florida Picks Up More *Fortune 500* Companies

Florida has never been a state with a large concentration of corporate headquarters like California, the home of Silicon Valley, New York, the country's financial capital, and Texas, the center of the energy industry. In the 2021 *Fortune 500* (based on financial data for 2020), California and New York tied for first place with 53 companies each, with Texas coming next with 49. Nevertheless, Florida continued to increase its share on the 2021 list, adding two companies and raising its ranking from 10th to 8th.[134]

Three Florida companies joined the list and one switched states. Carrier Global came in at no. 171. CHEWY, an Amazon for pets, joined at no. 403. Roper Technologies, a diversified technology company climbed up the list to 488. And Icahn Enterprises, which left New York for Florida, was no. 453.

This was offset by the loss of two Florida companies. Hertz Global Holdings, the car rental company, dropped off the list, falling to no. 508. And Tech Data, a company specializing in the global distribution of Information Technology products and services, was acquired, and merged with another IT company, Synnex, a California company. While the headquarters of the operation will no longer be in Florida, the scale of operations in Clearwater is not expected to be reduced.[135]

10
TOURISTS AND SNOWBIRDS FLOCK BACK

Tourism Takes a Beating and Keeps on Ticking

The tourism industry in the Sunshine State had a banner year in 2019, receiving a record 131.1 million visitors. More people than ever were being lured down by Florida's enchanting beaches and many beguiling attractions. *Laissez les bons temps rouler*, as the Cajuns say at Mardi Gras, was also the hope for 2020. But in March, Covid fears, stoked by the rapid buildup of cases from miniscule levels and doomsday projections of the number of cases and deaths in store, sent most visitors scurrying back to their homes, particularly if they were from Canada or overseas where borders were snapping shut. This sent the number of visitors plummeting to less than a third of the first quarter levels, which had already begun to sag merely on talk of Covid (Chart 26). And the number of Canadian and Overseas visitors dried up.

This was clearly an unsustainable situation for Florida, which counts on tourism to fuel much of its economy. Following the reopening of Florida starting in May and becoming more complete in September, the number of visits began to recover in the third quarter of the year. By the second half of-2021, the number of visitors had surpassed 2019 record levels. Still not so many Canadians and Overseas visitors yet, but the Americans were back in force coming in record numbers, many of whom probably came from Northeastern states that were still saddled by much greater Covid restraints.[136] For 2021 the number of visitors was 122.4 million, not quite as high as 2019, but still a remarkable comeback.

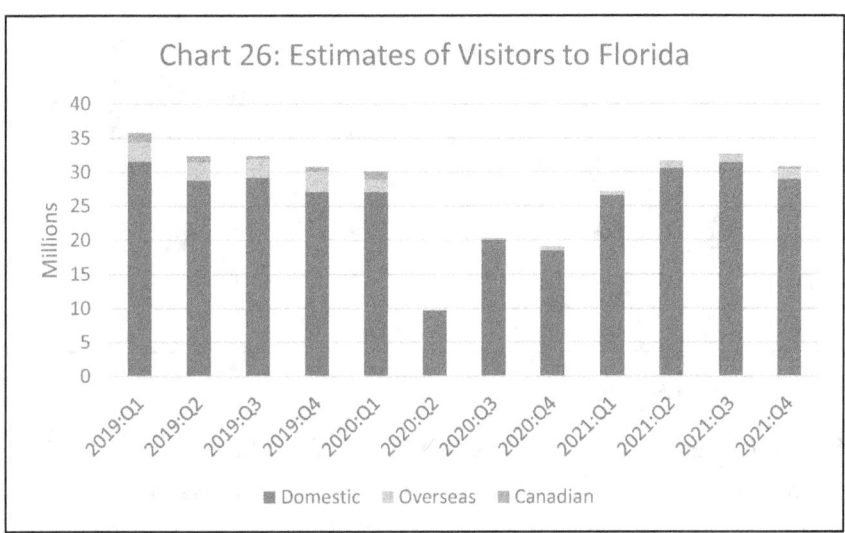

Source: VisitFlorida®.[137]

All the visitors to Florida need a place to stay. And shorter-term visitors usually choose hotels. The bottom fell out of the hotel accommodation industry in the second quarter of 2020 when the visitors all left. Hotel room nights sold plummeted to 40 percent of its first quarter level in the second quarter (Chart 27). The recovery started in the third quarter, but it wasn't until the second quarter of 2021 that nights sold almost got back to the level reached in the same quarters of 2019. Nevertheless, for the year 2021 as a whole, nights sold reached 110 million, which was only 6 ½ percent down from 2019.

With demand falling in the second quarter of 2020, the average daily rate in hotels dropped sharply from $168.03 to $96.85, which was an additional blow to hotel owners who were already reeling but was a real bargain for visitors not scared away by Covid (Chart 28). Hotel average daily rates increased as the visitors returned. By the fourth quarter of 2021 hotel average room rates were $162.89 or

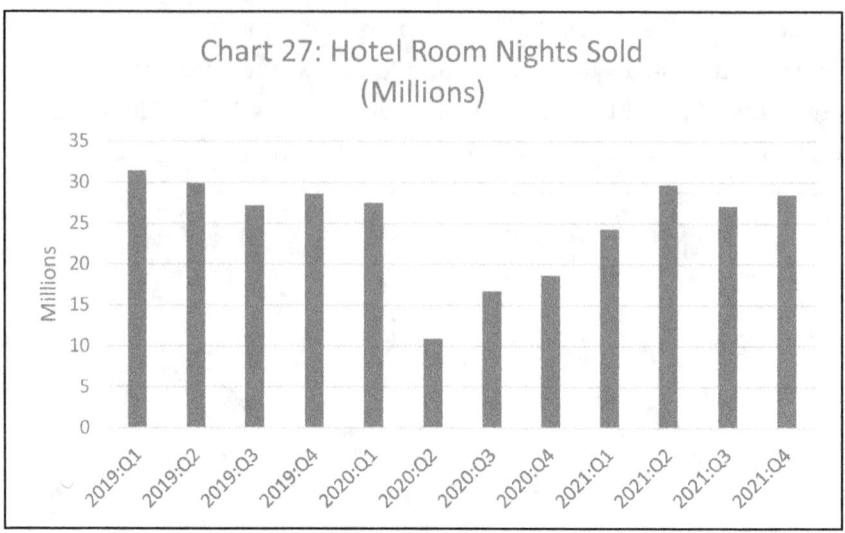

Source: VisitFlorida®.[138]

$23.38 higher than in the fourth quarter of 2019 before the pandemic started. This represents a 16.8-percent increase. Florida hoteliers are taking advantage of demand to make up for all of the revenues lost to Covid.

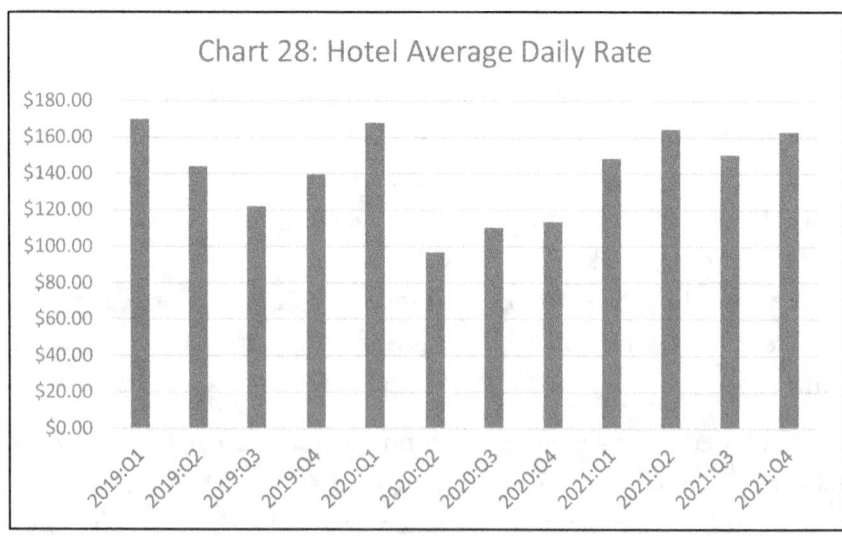

Source: VisitFlorida®.[139]

Canadians Took a Raincheck in the Winter of 2021

Most Canadians returned home after their government issued a travel advisory against international travel on March 13, 2020, calling them back. This travel advisory was taken very seriously by Canadian snowbirds, particularly because of its implications for their travel insurance. Several of the large Canadian insurance companies, including Manulife, Allianz, TuGo, and Blue Cross, stopped providing coverage against Covid for Canadians leaving Canada in defiance of the advisory. Another company cancelled all emergencymedical coverage of Canadians outside Canada after March 23 if they didn't skedaddle back home.[140] No Canadians wanted to end up in a U.S. hospital with Covid and bankrupt to boot.

This advisory was quickly followed by an agreement between Canada and the United States to close the land border between the two countries for all non-essential travel for tourism or recreation as of March 21, 2020.[141] This restriction on travel was extended monthly by the Canadian Government for more than 16 months until it was finally lifted as of August 9, 2021, for vaccinated Americans and permanent residents with a negative molecular Covid test.[142] The restriction on the U.S. side that prevented Canadians from crossing the land border to the United States lingered for another couple of months until November 8, 2021, when the U.S. border was finally opened to fully vaccinated Canadians.[143]

However, the U.S. border restraint on Canadians wasn't quite as tight as it appeared at first glance since it did not apply to air travel. Canadian snowbirds could still fly down, but just not come in their cars and RVs. Nevertheless, this was a real downer for Canadian snowbirds who like to drive their vehicles down to Florida. But capitalists are nothing if not enterprising, and it wasn't long before a new business sprang up to take advantage of the border loophole. Trucking companies, whose cross-border shipments were not controlled, quickly saw the opportunity to transport vehicles to nearby U.S. border cities. Canadians could then fly down and pick up their vehicles. The only drawback was the hefty additional cost, which could add up to a few thousand dollars. This rigmarole did not make a lot of sense to Canadian snowbirds who were stuck with the arbitrary extra cost, but some of them took advantage of it anyway.[144]

Only 1,358,00 Canadians visited Florida in 2020, a decline of 67 percent from the previous year. More tellingly, only a meager 114 thousand of these came after March when the Canadian Government issued its travel advisory, shutting the border for tourists. In 2021, only 584 thousand Canadians managed to make it to Florida and most of them came in the final quarter of the year.[145]

The allure of Florida to our northern neighbors was still strong when they were given the opportunity to come down after the border finally opened on November 7, 2021. Canadian snowbirds anxious to beat the rush lined up to cross the border at midnight on that long-awaited day like pioneers for a land rush. One Canadian, who I know, told me he managed to come across in light traffic at 2 a.m. All that day there was a steady stream of traffic headed south from Canada.[146] Many must have made it to Florida. In our town, the Canadians are back. This winter, unlike last, they are free to enjoy the warm, sunny Florida winter, and once again send their friends, back in the land of ice and snow, postcards of palm-tree framed beaches.

A recent article in the *Montreal Gazette* by Canadian humorist Josh Freed captures the schizophrenic attraction-repulsion Canadians have for the Sunshine State in the time of Covid, especially in the winter when the usual gloom from a surfeit of ice and snow in Canada is further depressed by some of the tightest Covid restrictions in the world. Seeking a break from the dreariness of his Covid-obsessed home province of Quebec like many Canadians, Freed jumped at the opportunity to escape to Florida, which to him on arriving seemed like "another planet" where people didn't wear masks and worry about Covid all the time. He wryly observed that it was "easy to spot Canadians at restaurants, as we're the ones properly masked and nervously sitting on the terrace, even in the rain."[147] Freed's humor wasn't much appreciated by many dour Canadians and Floridians, who drowned him under a tidal wave of criticism for daring to satirize their differing approaches to Covid.[148] But at least bashing his article did give many Canadians an opportunity to let off steam after being cooped up for so long by Covid.

It's the frustration with Covid restrictions that drove the Canadian trucker's "Freedom Convoy" carrying 10,000 protestors rockin' through the night to converge on Parliament Hill in Ottawa on the weekend of January 29-30, 2022.[149] Evidently, there are some Canadians that would prefer the Florida approach to dealing with Covid if they were given a choice.

Disney Parks in Orlando Take a Punch and Get Up

When the Walt Disney Company, Florida's largest employer with 77,000 workers, shut down its Orlando parks on March 12, 2020, because of the outbreak of Covid, it dealt a staggering blow to the Florida economy.[150] This was a costly, but probably unavoidable, decision for Disney. According to company executives, shutting down all its theme parks around the world cost almost $5 billion in lost revenue in April, May, and June of that year.[151] Much of this revenue would have come from its Orlando parks, which are its top money makers.

Disney was lucky that so many of its parks were in Florida though. After July 1, they were allowed to reopen, albeit at only at 25 percent capacity. The Magic Kingdom and Animal Kingdom opened July 11, and EPCOT and Hollywood Studios on July 15. All guests had to wear masks and have their temperature taken prior to entering. In November, the company raised the capacity ceiling to 35 percent reflecting its own estimates of the safe capacity of the park, again allowing for social distancing and masking.

Nevertheless, 2020 was an *annus horribilis* for Disney's Orlando Parks. The four most popular theme parks at Walt Disney World – the Magic Kingdom, Animal Kingdom, EPCOT, and Hollywood

Studios – only received 18.8 million visitors, a 68 percent decrease from 2019.[152]

Again, on May 17, 2021, the Disney Company raised the capacity limit again by an unspecified amount.[153] While guests didn't have to be vaccinated, they were required to wear a mask in indoor locations and enclosed transportation and even on some rides. It wasn't until August 18, 2021, that face coverings were made optional in outdoor areas.[154] Evidently Disney still had a problem shaking its California state of mind and getting on with the Florida program. It was only on November 22 that Disney followed Florida law and dropped the vaccine requirement it was trying to impose on its employees.[155]

While the data isn't available yet, the available evidence suggest that attendance at Disney parks increased substantially in 2021 especially late in the year around Thanksgiving and the Holiday Season, and that this has continued into 2022 with big crowds for the Martin Luther King Day weekend.[156] Hopefully, this is the light at the end of the tunnel.

Disneyland and its sister park California Adventures in Anaheim, California lost many more customers percentagewise in 2020 than the Orlando Disney Complex. The reason is simple: they were completely shut down after March 14, 2020, because of Covid for the rest of the year and into 2021.[157] Consequently, attendance at these two California Disney parks tanked 80.3 percent in 2020 to only 5.6 million visitors or less than 30 percent of the number at the four most popular Florida parks. Then after reopening on April 30, 2021, Disneyland was subject to a 25 percent capacity limit. It was only on June 15, 2021, after the state opened that the parks were allowed to return to their normal operations at 100 percent capacity. Even so, unlike in Florida, they were subject to a vaccination requirement.[158]

The Cruise Industry Encounters Heavy Seas

Florida is the center of the U.S. cruise industry, which operates out of the five ports of Miami, Port Canaveral, Port Everglades,

Jacksonville, and Tampa. In 2019 with a record 8.3 million cruise embarkations, 36.4 percent above 2012 levels, Florida ports accounted for 60 percent of total U.S. embarkations.[159]

The cruise industry was almost sunk by Covid. The media was filled in the spring of 2020 with horror stories about cruise ship passengers and crew, already at sea and confined to their cabins or quarters, on ships where people were sick with Covid or even dying, while their ships desperately sought ports willing to receive them and provide treatment.[160] After that, the CDC didn't need to tell most people that "The chance of getting COVID-19 on cruise ships is high because the virus spreads easily between people in close quarters aboard ships," but it did anyway because that's its job.[161]

The CDC issued a No Sail Order prohibiting cruise ships from taking passengers from U.S. ports as of March 14, 2020. These orders were extended monthly while the CDC focused on controlling Covid on ships still at sea and preventing returning passengers from spreading Covid. On October 1, 2020, the CDC released a Framework for Conditional Sailing Order, which involved establishing and assessing an elaborate set of measures designed to counter Covid at sea and to prepare the industry for eventually reopening. It too kept being extended and refined but seemed to never get to the point of allowing cruise ships back to sea with paying passengers.[162]

In the spring 2021, the Cruise Lines Industry Association and the State of Florida voiced their growing frustration with the slow-moving process and argued that the Conditional Sailing Order did not "reflect the industry's proven advancements and success operating in other parts of the world, nor the advent of vaccines."[163] Governor DeSantis became increasingly exasperated by the CDC's foot-dragging and the reluctance to allow cruising to start up again. Major cruise companies like Crystal Cruises, Celebrity, Royal Caribbean announced cruises from new homeports all around the world with laxer requirements. Losing patience and worrying about losing out on cruises, Governor DeSantis launched a legal action against the U.S. Government in early April 2021.[164] On June 18, the U.S. district court in Tampa blocked the application of the CDC's restrictions to cruise ships operating from Florida ports, thus freeing the Florida industry to resume passenger operations. This ruling was allowed to stand when on July 23, 2021, the Eleventh Circuit Court of Appeals refused to issue a stay pending an appeal to the Supreme Court.[165] Consequently, the Conditional Sailing Order now only applies to foreign-flagged ships and becomes "non-binding recommendations" for ships operating from Florida ports.[166]

On July 28, 2021, the Royal Caribbean's *Celebrity Edge* departed Port Everglades to become the first cruise ship in over 15 months to leave on a cruise from an U.S. port. It only carried 1,100 passengers or slightly more than a third of its 3,000 capacity.[167]

The Florid cruise industry was worth fighting for. It is a bulwark of the Florida tourism economy. In 2019 before Covid, the industry accounted for direct spending of $9 billion and 159 thousand jobs earning a total income of $8.1 billion.[168]

However, the cruise industry is not out of the rough water yet. It has also been afflicted by the outbreak of the more contagious, but thankfully less lethal, Omicron variant and the CDC has warned again against cruise ship travel.[169] Ports of call have been closed because of Covid restrictions. Many passengers have been deterred from going on cruises because of Covid concerns. And voyages have had to be cancelled by the likes of Royal Caribbean and Celebrity.[170]

That the cruise industry is not faring well was illustrated by the recent escapade of the Crystal *Symphony*, which was diverted to the Bahamas after a U.S. court ordered that it be seized to pay its unpaid $4.6 million fuel bill. The passengers were not pleased to be dumped in Bimini and forced to take a rough ferry ride to Port Everglades. It's also not a good sign for the industry's financial health that Crystal has suspended operations for two of its ships and its river cruises.[171]

11
REAL ESTATE BOOMS

Home building was a sector of the economy that was not kept down by Covid for long. And the initial weakness in house construction turned into a boom with house prices soaring.

Building Permits for Housing Bounce Back

Building permits for housing units initially declined after Covid, falling 17.7 percent from March to April of 2020, probably because of uncertainty about the future and concerns over Covid (Chart 29). However, this was nothing compared to the more than 90 percent collapse that occurred from September 2005 to March 2009 during the Florida housing bust. More importantly, the decrease in 2020 was short lived and quickly reversed as the Federal Government introduced stimulus programs and the Federal Reserve increased the money supply and lowered interest rates. With 30-year mortgage rates dropping from 3.5 percent at the beginning of March 2020 to 2.65 percent by the beginning of January 2021,[172] the monthly mortgage payments on a home became much more affordable. By November 21, 2021, building permits had risen a whopping 35.8 per cent from March 2020 levels.

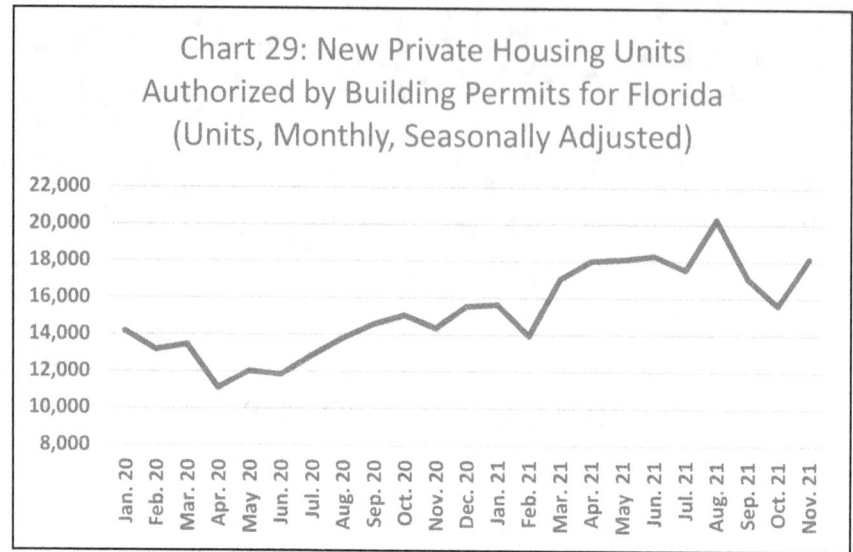

Source: U.S. Census Bureau.[173]

House Prices Take Off

According to data published by the St. Louis Federal Reserve Bank, the demand for housing since the onset of Covid pushed the house price index for Florida up by almost 25 percent from January 2020 to July 2021 (Chart 30). Over this period, the rate of increase picked up in 2021. The fiscal and monetary stimulus introduced to keep the economy afloat during Covid combined with population growth buoyed housing permits to levels not seen since early 2006 before Florida housing prices collapsed, and propelled housing prices to new highs above even those reached at the peak of the last housing price bubble. This will make a move to Florida less affordable, especially for retirees on fixed incomes. Overheated is the word to describe the current Florida housing market.

California and New York benefitted from the same fiscal and monetary stimulus, but their housing prices did not rise as much as in Florida. In California housing prices only increased 19.4 percent January 2020 to July 2021 and New York only 16.7.[174] This might have been because of the population declines experienced by these two states while Florida was growing. But who would have ever guessed that Covid would have stoked a real estate boom even in states losing population?

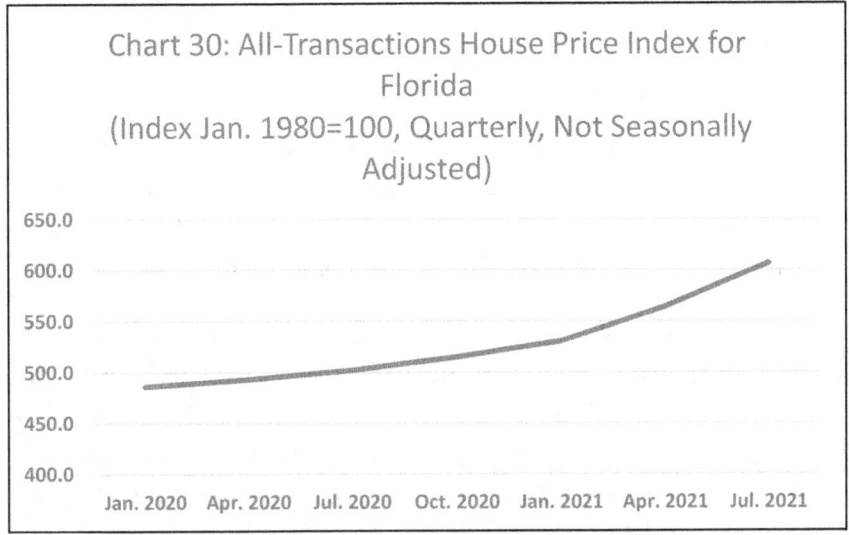

Source: U.S. Federal Housing Finance Agency.[175]

Master Planned Communities (MPCs)

A Master-Planned Community is a unified development incorporating homes, stores, restaurants, and recreational amenities like swimming pools, golf courses, tennis courts, and parks and offering a wide range of services such as clinics and schools. It has become a particularly popular form of urban development in Florida where retirees pine for the old-fashioned small towns of yore.

A real estate consulting firm called RCLCO does an annual survey of the top selling MPCs nationwide. The latest covered the first half of 2021 and was published in July 2021.[176] In this survey, thirteen of the top 50 MPCs were in Florida, and they accounted for 34 percent of total sales. From the first half of 2020 to the first half of 2021, sales of units in these Florida MPCs increased 29.2 percent, which was 9 percent higher than the total for all 50 MPCs on the list.

The top two MPCs were both located in Florida: Lakewood Ranch in Sarasota, and The Villages. Lakewood Ranch experienced an astonishing 83.2 percent increase. The other four most rapidly growing MPCs, all of which recorded increases of 70 percent or more, were: no. 15 Top of the World in Ocala; no. 24 the Catholic community of Ave Maria; no. 27 Epperson in Wesley Chapel; and no. 31 eTown in Jacksonville.

These MPCs are reshaping the Florida landscape. Two examples are Lake Nona and Babcock Ranch, not because they are the biggest, Lake Nona only is no. 19 on the list and Babcock Ranch no. 25, but because of their future potential and innovative nature.

Lake Nona is a community outside Orlando. Over the last twenty years it has grown to house around 70,000 people. In addition to the usual, it features USTA's new tennis facility, which with its one hundred tennis courts is the largest in the world, as well as a new Medical City that already houses research facilities and the University of Central Florida's College of Medicine and the Burnett School of Biomedical Sciences. A new development that has big implications for Lake Nona is Disney's plans to move 2,000 workers there from California over the next eighteen months or so. That will really supercharge the local housing market as these people will all need homes.[177] And more people may be on the way.

Babcock Ranch is a greenfield development on 17,000 acres in Charlotte County. Since this is where I live, it is convenient to drop by from time to time to see how it's coming. Situated on scrub pasture, farmed, and rock mined land that used to belong to a cattle ranch, the land to be developed is surrounded by pine flatwoods. At its center on the shores of Lake Babcock, one of its many lakes, is a hometown providing services like restaurants, stores, schools, a clinic, and town offices. Babcock Ranch prides itself on being plugged in to a fiber optic network and being solar powered with 870 acres of solar panels operated by Florida Power & Light.

In early 2018, when its first residents moved in, there were only a few lonely houses and the town infrastructure for a planned city of

50,000 inhabitants. By December 2019, 500 homes had been constructed. Despite Covid, another 500 were built in 2020 and 700 in 2021. Production is ramping up by nine home builders, including Lennar, Pulte, and D.R. Holton. The development looks like it is well on track to meet its target of 19,000 homes by build out in 20 years.[178]

12
LARGE PROJECTS MOVE AHEAD

Construction of some big projects slowed down because of Covid. But this was only temporary for most. By 2021 construction had resumed. Two of the three projects reviewed in my earlier book *Florida Dreams* are progressing.[179] The exception is the American Dreams Mall in Miami-Dade County.

Water Street Tampa on Track

Construction on the $3.5 billion Water Street project in Tampa to renew the downtown waterfront, which commenced in 2018, continued through Covid. Completion of Phase I of the project is slated for 2022. Characterized as America's largest urban redevelopment project, it has already begun leasing commercial and residential space, which will eventually include one million square feet for offices, one million retail and cultural, 3,500 residential units. It will also have over 1,400 new and renovated hotel rooms. The place is already a cornucopia of restaurants and fast-food outlets.[180] By 2027 when Phase II is scheduled for completion, this development will double the size of downtown Tampa, giving the city a downtown core worthy of the Twenty-First Century.[181]

The Sunseeker Resort Rises from the Ashes

A large structure can be seen going up right across the Peace River from my town of Punta Gorda. It is the Sunseeker Resort in Charlotte Harbor, a $510 million project undertaken by Allegiant

Airlines. When finished, it will be a huge resort complex with five hundred hotel rooms, 180 extended stay suites, two swimming pools, 19 cafes, restaurants and bars, and a nearby exclusive redesigned golf course. Upon completion, it's expected to employ 500 people and accommodate 300,000 tourists a year.[182]

In mid-March Allegiant caught workers by surprise when, because of Covid, it told contractors to stop work, putting four hundred out of a job.[183] And then not long after the Covid lockdown ended in mid-May, Allegiant announced more ominously that the project was being "suspended indefinitely."[184]

The mammoth partially complete concrete shell of Sunseeker with six huge cranes perched on top loomed menacingly over US 41 for seventeen months and through two hurricane seasons, while speculation in the local community ran amuck. Everyone knew that Allegiant was facing financial difficulties because of the Covid-induced collapse in airline travel and that it couldn't afford to proceed with the project. Many wondered if the site would sit abandoned for years as an eyesore until all the exposed rebar corroded due to the salt air and the completed work deteriorated becoming worthless.

Wild rumors circulated. People claimed to have sighted Arab sheiks in thawbs in Punta Gorda and wondered if they were inspecting the site as a possible investment. People speculated that Seminole Indians were trying to buy the unfinished resort to make it into a casino. And when you thought it couldn't get any stranger, the scuttlebutt had Tom Cruise jetting into town to investigate the possibility of turning the resort into a Scientology training center like in Clearwater. None of these fantasies was ever substantiated.

Then in August 2021, just when everyone was beginning to give up hope, some small-scale activity was seen on the site. Then Allegiant President John Redmond announced that construction had started up at the beginning of the month and that it had always been their plan to resume in 18 months.[185] Sunseekers is now expected to be finished by late 2022 or early 2023.[186] This is another indication that the recovery in the tourism industry is well underway.

Miami's American Dream Mall May Be an Exception

Not all major projects have been able to rebound from Covid. The American Dream Mall in Miami-Dade is a $4 billion mega-project that was planned by the Triple Five Group, a company controlled by the Ghermezian family which made their name developing the West Edmonton Mall and the Mall of the Americas in Minnesota outside of the twin cities of Minneapolis-St. Paul. It was originally scheduled for completion at the end of 2021 and was to be built in Miami-Dade County at the intersection of I-75 and the Florida Turnpike near the Broward County line. Like its sister malls, it was to be a tourist destination, drawing people from all over the world to enjoy its many attractions, including a water park, submarine ride, skating rink, and ski hill. The visitors would also have more than a thousand stores to shop in and dozens of restaurants for their dining pleasure.

The Florida American Dream Mall was preceded by another smaller scale, but still giant, sister American Dream Mall that was completed in late 2019 ten miles outside of New York City. Its timing couldn't have been worse. After Covid struck, that mall was forced to shut for almost six months. This undermined its financial viability and led the developer to default on the $1.2 billion construction loan, which cost the Triple Five Group 49 percent of the equity in its other two big malls that had been put up as collateral for the loan. In addition, because of Covid, malls across the country have been losing business as shoppers have shifted to online retailers, most notably Amazon. These developments cast a large shadow over the American Dream Mall in Miami that could compromise its ability to secure financing. Its scheduled late 2026 opening looks increasingly like a pipe dream.[187]

Skyscrapers Are Going Up in Miami

Glass and steel towers are sprouting like mushrooms again. Concerns over Covid and the desire of employees to work at home posed no barrier to a renewed construction boom in Southeast Florida. In 2021, there were twenty-one new tall buildings under construction.

They ranged from the 818-feet Aston Martin Residences, which will be the tallest residential building south of New York City, to the Yotelpad, a 31 stories condo and hotel development.[188] The 50-story office tower at 830 Brickell is already leasing trophy office space to companies wanting to be at the center of the action in the financial center of Latin America, when it opens in 2022. Microsoft was one of the companies taking a lease on 50,000 square feet of space.[189]

Non-Residential and Residential Construction Spending Both Strong

While there was a 7.6 percent decline in real GDP in construction from the first quarter of 2020 to the second after Covid struck, it soon rebounded so that by the fourth quarter it was above pre-covid levels (Chart 31). For the 2020 year, including both residential and nonresidential, construction, it averaged about $45.43 billion, down only $30 million from 2019. In 2021, real GDP in construction was above 2019 levels in the first three quarters of the year.

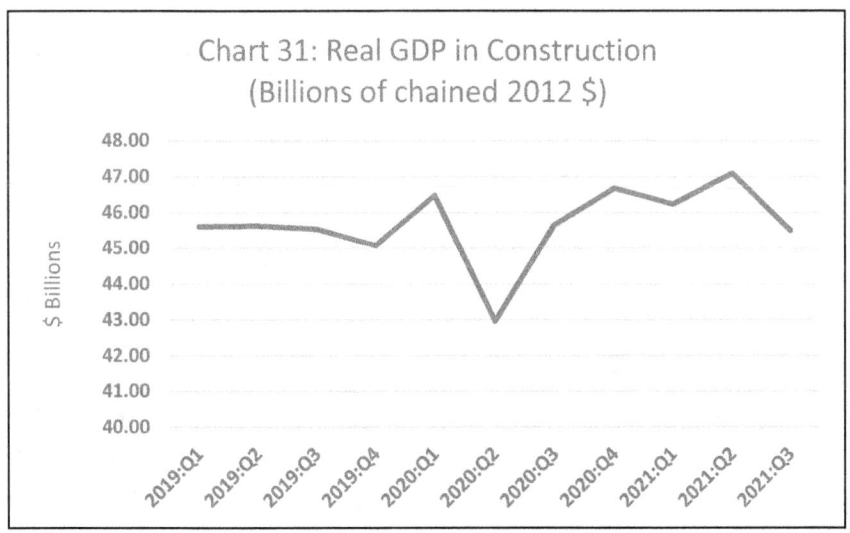

Source: Bureau of Economic Analysis, Regional Data.[190]

With a decline of 2.1 per cent in real GDP in construction from the first quarter of 2020 to the third quarter, Florida ranked 32nd among the fifty states and the District of Columbia giving it a weak performance in construction (Chart 32). The other two blue Mega-states both had better performances. New York had the strongest performance at 2.3 percent, followed by California at -0.5 percent. Covid restrictions did not stand in the way of the recovery of the construction industry in these states. Construction in Texas, which decreased 2.2 percent, was slightly weaker than in Florida.

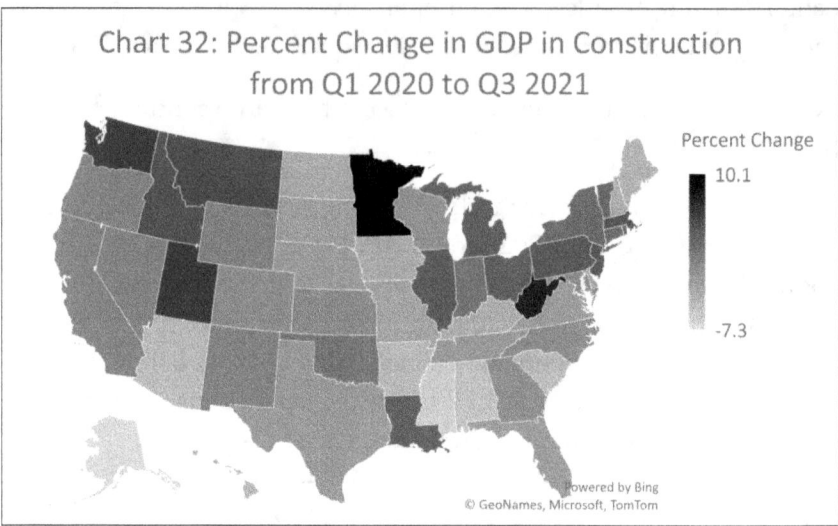

Source: Bureau of Economic Analysis, Regional Data.[191]

13
FLORIDA DREAMS LIVE ON

Covid has eroded many of the freedoms that Americans have long cherished and that our founding fathers enshrined in our constitution. At first, it was widely accepted that some curtailments of our liberties were necessary to protect us from the deadly new disease about which little was known, and much was feared. Into that information vacuum, Dr. Anthony Fauci stepped to become the nation's chief Covid guru. His pronouncements were embraced by governments and became policy across the land regardless of how many times he contradicted himself. Based on the White House Coronavirus Task Force and CDC guidelines, the necessity of which were accepted on faith by state governments and indeed most Americans, the largest government intervention in our nation's history was launched. It was on a scale unparalleled in the past even under totalitarian governments.

Non-essential businesses were shut down across the country. Schools, churches, museums, libraries, restaurants, bars, gyms, movie theaters, sporting events, concerts, barber shops, hairdressers, other personal service businesses, and you name it were all shuttered. Masks (including the designer cloth kind that don't work as well as the N-95 that do) became mandatory or at least de rigueur, even outside. Hand washing with both soap and water and ever-present sanitizers was pursued obsessively to the point where people rubbed the skin off their hands leaving sores. Six-foot social distancing (two meters in the rest of the world including Canada) was religiously applied even to the point of requiring people treating friends like lepers. That the elderly were more vulnerable made it imperative that they be cut off from their families out of fear of Covid and made to feel isolated and lonely. And surfaces, including even grocery products, were routinely scrubbed free of germs until it became clear to even the most gullible that this did nothing to prevent Covid.

After a month or so of these obsessions, most Floridians had had enough and were ready to move on and get on with their lives. Indeed, many had no choice but to do so because they had to go back out in the world to earn a living. The structure of the Florida economy with tourism bulking so large left many no option to stay home and work remotely as there was for many better-paid high technology, finance, and government sector workers in states like New York and California.

While at the beginning Governor DeSantis, like everybody else, accepted the need for drastic emergency measures to slow the spread, he recognized that Florida could not remain locked down for long without irreparably damaging the state's economy and society. His intuition was sound and was confirmed by the recent Johns Hopkins study published in January 2022.[192] In effect, the cure, even if it worked, which we now know it didn't, could not be allowed to become worse than the disease. As any economist will tell you, it is always necessary to make trade-offs. Keeping everything shut might have reduced Covid a little (even if nobody can tell you by how much). But it also would have cost Floridians their jobs, their incomes, their educations, and their general welfare and overall satisfaction with life.

The Governor had to act, and, to his credit, did so decisively, guided by the science and observing the law. Under his stewardship Florida became a leader showing other states how they could open up while still dealing responsibly with Covid and safeguarding the health of their residents and guests to the extent possible. A key element in his approach was emphasizing the personal responsibility of Floridians to make their own health decisions. But this was balanced by the specific public health measures that were introduced by his administration. For instance, the state's most vulnerable population was protected by the establishment of special nursing centers to segregate the elderly with Covid and thus prevent the disease from rampaging through nursing homes and assisted living facilities like in New York. An innovative public-private partnership with Publix and other pharmacies was set up to administer Covid vaccinations and overcome bureaucratic bottlenecks in distribution, which was hampering the vaccines rollout. Through the Florida Department of Health and Florida Division of Emergency Management, the state government also oversaw the establishment of testing sites across the state. More recently, Governor DeSantis championed the distribution of monoclonal antibodies, a new treatment administered intravenously even though on this he was eventually thwarted by the FDA, evidently with the approval of the Biden Administration.

The most distinctive aspect of Florida's Covid response in comparison to that in Democratic states is how fast the state was opened at the end of the lockdown. It was this that made Governor DeSantis a favorite target of progressives. Starting at the end of April 2000 the various restrictions were removed in phases until by the end of September most were gone. By fall normal life had returned and restaurants and bars were filled with people enjoying themselves, while up north people were forced to dine outside shivering in the cold. At the start of the 2020-21 school year in August, all the students, who so chose, could go back to the classroom for in-person learning subject to a mask requirement. Meanwhile in many Northeast and West Coast states students were still being educated remotely and spending long hours straining their eyes gazing at computer screens. For the 2021-22 school year in Florida, the mask requirement was completely gone by law.

Florida's openness, so decried by progressives, became its greatest asset. Out-of-state visitors came from locked down blue states not only for the sunshine and beaches as always but to enjoy the freedom of a return to a more normal life without all the irksome constraints of Covid.

Representative Alexandria Ocasio-Cortez, of woke Democratic Squad fame, was not the only politician from a state with draconian Covid policies to frolic maskless in the Sunshine State. Her much-reported appearance prompted Governor DeSantis to joke "If I had a dollar for every lockdown politician who decided to escape to Florida over the last two years, I'd be a pretty doggone wealthy man, let me tell you."[193]

Unlike AOC, some out-of-state visitors even stay for longer periods because of the option of working remotely and maybe even enroll their children in Florida's open schools. After a while, some might even decide that the time had come to make the move. And it wouldn't take many bringing their businesses along to give a real boost to the Florida economy.

Florida's enhanced appeal due to its openness is confirmed by the enormous number of new arrivals in Florida since Covid, 305,218 to be exact over the April 1, 2020, to July 1, 2021, period. This testifies to the strength of Florida Dreams. The downside for the blue Mega-states of California and New York is that people are leaving them in droves.

While population growth fuels the Florida economy, it will also put additional pressure on Florida's fragile environment. Even though progress is being made on restoring the water flows through the Everglades under the Comprehensive Everglades Restoration Plan, much more work needs to be done to restore and protect Florida's land and water, which have always been the state's greatest attractions and resources. The restored flow through the glades is necessary to clean the water and replenish the water table in Southeast Florida. It will also reduce the need to dump the phosphate-rich water of Lake Okeechobee into the two rivers flowing out, thus feeding the red tide and blue-green algae blooms that pollute our coastal water and beaches and kill our fish and other marine animals and birds on both coasts.[194] While not believed to be the cause of last summer's red tide, a leak from the Piney Point fertilizer plant's reservoir pond detected in late March also could have fed it and cyanobacteria blooms around Tampa Bay.[195] In January 2022 more leaks were detected, which shows that the situation has yet to be fully remedied.[196] This should sound an alarm about the possible existence of other industrial sites around the state that need attention on a proactive basis.

Covid is not just going to go away magically, returning life everywhere back to as it was. Even before the Omicron variant exploded, Dr. Fauci acknowledged that "we're going to have to start "living with COVID."[197] This could be interpreted charitably as confirming his conversion to an approach that had been pioneered by Governor DeSantis.

We must face the unpleasant facts. Covid may persist for a long time. It may even never be eradicated and become a permanent feature like the seasonal flu or colds, but worse, with every variant having a different Greek letter name until the alphabet is exhausted (except for Xi, of course, to avoid offending China's paramount leader). Therapeutics like monoclonal antibodies and antivirals, and new anti-viral treatments like the Pfizer's Paxlovid and Merck's Molnupiravir pills can alleviate the disease, but not wipe it out. Nevertheless, the anti-virals, because they are pills that can be taken at home, have been described as "gamechangers" because they keep people out of hospitals and avoid overloading them with a burden of critically sick patients that can't be handled and that displace other people who need care.[198] It's too bad the Biden Administration didn't arrange for a bulk purchase in the summer of 2020 when Pfizer announced its product similarly to the way the Trump Administration did for the vaccine. If it had done so, hospitals wouldn't be as full as they are in early 2022 because of Omicron.

Given this possibility, or even likelihood, it should be clear that we can't remain cloistered forever, and that we need to get on with our lives. That may be why Florida has become a beacon of freedom to so many just wanting to live.[199]

It may not only be the openness of Florida that makes it so attractive, but the continued adherence of so many of its citizens to traditional American values. Critical race theory, which is contrary to many of these values and is abhorrent to many Floridians, has not yet taken deep root in Florida like it has in many blue states, where it fuels racial tensions and promotes anti-Americanism. However, to make sure it never does, Governor DeSantis has passed the "Stop WOKE Act," which bans it from Florida's schools and corporations and gives citizens the tools to make sure it isn't rammed down their throats unwillingly.[200]

Florida was not swept up in all the demonize and defund-the-police nonsense following the killing of George Floyd. The police are still respected and allowed to do their job of keeping Floridians safe. That's why law enforcement is still a desirable profession in Florida. People moving down know they will be secure and that rioting, and looting will not be tolerated in their cities.

New Virginia Governor Glenn Youngkin was swept into office in January 2022 on a wave of voter dissatisfaction with the treatment of parents by the overbearing Loudon County School Board with the tacit support of the U.S. Attorney General who requested that local offices of the Department of Justice convene meetings to look into threats against school boards.[201] Delivering on his promises, Governor Youngkin issued a slew of executive orders after being sworn into office. The first prohibited the use of the divisive concept of critical race theory in the schools, and the second banned mask mandates,[202] both of which are policies already adopted in Florida. It is encouraging to see such policies also attracting support in other states. Governor DeSantis has done a lot to rekindle the fires of liberty and equality in our country.

Florida dreams about living in the free and open state of Florida are American dreams. They are rooted in our desire to live our lives as free men and women not subject to all the restrictions imposed by an overbearing government quixotically fighting to eradicate a pandemic that has become an endemic.

ABOUT THE AUTHOR

PATRICK GRADY is a retired economist living in Punta Gorda,  Florida. He has a Ph.D. in economics from the University of Toronto and an A.B. from the University of Illinois. Over a lengthy career, he worked as a central banker, public servant, and economic consultant. To keep busy in Punta Gorda, he taught economics at Florida Southwestern State College for a few years.

Patrick has written many articles and five books on economic and fiscal issues, including most notably: *The Economic Consequences of Quebec Sovereignty* (Fraser Institute,1991); *Dividing the House: Preparing for a Canada without Quebec* (Harper Collins Canada, 1995) with Alan Freeman; *Seattle and Beyond: The WTO Millennium Round* (1999) with Katie Macmillan; and *Florida Dreams: All About the Amazing Rise of the Sunshine Mega-State* (2019). This current book picks up where *Florida Dreams* left off.

As a consultant, Patrick has worked for governments and corporations across Canada, and for the World Bank, the IMF, the U.S. Department of the Treasury, the United Nations, and the Asian Development Bank, in more than thirty-five countries in Europe, Asia, Africa, Latin America and the Caribbean.

Those not so hooked on the dismal science may be interested to hear that Patrick has also penned three novels. The first about the Vietnam War is *Through the Picture Tube* (Robert D. Reed Publishers, 2000). The second called *The Jade Head* (Robert D. Reed Publishers, 2004), his favorite, is an adventure story that takes place in Belize. The third, *Royal Canadian Jihad*, is about the threat of Islamic terrorism in Canada.

Most recently, Patrick published *A Yankee-Canuck Looks Back: One*

Damn Thing After Another (2020), in which he contemplates the meaning of his life.

Ironically, when he was finishing this present book on how Florida dealt with Covid-19, he finally got it and tested positive for the virus. Fortunately, though, perhaps because he was fully vaccinated and boosted, his case was asymptomatic. This gave him the opportunity to use his time in quarantine to polish off this book, free of the usual interruptions, except from his wife, who had to be taken care of because of the Covid she'd caught from an unknown source.

ENDNOTES

[1] "Pennsylvania Assembly: Reply to the Governor, 11 November 1755," Founders Online, National Archives.
<https://founders.archives.gov/documents/Franklin/01-06-02-0107>

[2] Emily Crane, "NIH admits US funded gain-of-function in Wuhan — despite Fauci's denials, *New York* Post, October 21, 2021.
<https://nypost.com/2021/10/21/nih-admits-us-funded-gain-of-function-in-wuhan-despite-faucis-repeated-denials/>

[3] There will never be incontrovertible evidence whether Covid came from the Wuhan Institute of Virology's laboratory or the nearby wet market because the Chinese government has stonewalled and refused to cooperate with independent international investigations, thus blocking access to the required information. This is pretty good evidence of culpability. But even without conclusive evidence one way or the other, there is still much controversy in the scientific community. See Amy Maxmen and Smriti Mallapaty, "The COVID lab-leak hypothesis: what scientists do and don't know," *Nature*, June 8, 2021. < https://www.nature.com/articles/d41586-021-01529-3 >; World Health Organization, "WHO-convened global study of origins of SARS-CoV-2: China Part," (2021). <https://bit.ly/3wjUXze>; Michael Worobey, "Dissecting the early COVID-19 cases in Wuhan, Science," *Science*, November 18, 2021.< https://www.science.org/doi/10.1126/science.abm4454> June 8, 2021.

[4] World Health Organization, "Listings of WHO's response to COVID-19," June 29, 2020. <https://www.who.int/news/item/29-06-2020-covidtimeline>

[5] Center for Disease Control, "First Travel-related Case of 2019 Novel Coronavirus Detected in United States, Press Release, January 21, 2020. <https://www.cdc.gov/media/releases/2020/p0121-novel-coronavirus-travel-case.html >

[6] Basavaraju, Sridhar V et al., "Serologic Testing of US Blood Donations to Identify Severe Acute Respiratory Syndrome Coronavirus 2 (SARS-CoV-2)–Reactive Antibodies: December 2019–January 2020," Clinical Infectious Diseases, Volume 72, Issue 12, June 15, 2021.
<https://academic.oup.com/cid/article/72/12/e1004/6012472>

[7] Joe Biden, "Statement from Vice President Joe Biden on Donald Trump's Expanded Travel Ban," February 1, 2020.
<https://medium.com/@JoeBiden/statement-from-vice-president-joe-biden-on-donald-trumps-expanded-travel-ban-17ac0ee039b9>
<https://twitter.com/JoeBiden/status/1223807268703043588> Later President Biden saw no problem with imposing a ban of his own on African countries. Myah Ward, "Biden admin announces travel ban for South Africa and 7 other countries, citing new variant," *Politico*, November 21,

2021.<https://www.politico.com/news/2021/11/26/biden-admin-announces-travel-ban-for-south-africa-and-7-other-countries-citing-new-variant-523394>

⁸ The study that got the most publicity was that done by Neil Ferguson and his team at the Imperial College London, which was picked up by the *New York Times*. Using epidemiological modelling, it projected that 81 percent of the U.S. population would get Covid in 2020 and 2.2 million would die if effective Non-Pharmaceutical Intervention mitigation strategies weren't adopted. Neil Ferguson et al., "Report 9: Impact of non-pharmaceutical interventions (NPIs) to reduce COVID-19 mortality and healthcare demand," March 16, 2020, p.7. <file:///C:/Users/P_Gra/Documents/Florida%20Book%202/Imperial-College-COVID19-NPI-modelling-16-03-2020.pdf>

⁹ Jon Campbell, "Andrew Cuomo's COVID book deal is worth $5 million, new tax records show," *Democrat & Chronicle*, May 17, 2021. <https://www.democratandchronicle.com/story/news/2021/05/17/andrew-cuomo-covid-books-how-much-paid/5125721001/>

¹⁰ Rachel Cohrs, "Andrew Cuomo's Covid-19 nursing home fiasco shows the ethical perils of pandemic policymaking," *Stat*, February 26, 2021. <https://www.statnews.com/2021/02/26/cuomos-nursing-home-fiasco-ethical-perils-pandemic-policymaking/>; C. Van Houtven, et al. "State Policy Responses to COVID-19 in Nursing Homes," *Journal of Long-Term Care* (2021), pp. 264–282. < https://doi.org/10.31389/jltc.81>

¹¹ Florida, Office of the Governor, Executive Order 20-112, (Phase 1: Safe. Smart. Step-by-Step. Plan for Florida's Recovery), April 29, 2020. <https://www.flgov.com/wp-content/uploads/orders/2020/EO_20-112.pdf>

¹² Jeffrey S. Solochek, "Appellate court overturns temporary injunction in school reopening lawsuit," *Tampa Bay Times*, October 9, 2020. <https://www.tampabay.com/news/education/2020/10/09/appellate-court-overturns-temporary-injunction-in-school-reopening-lawsuit/>

¹³ Russell Redman, "Publix set to begin coronavirus vaccinations in Florida: Gov. Ron DeSantis announces pilot with Southeast grocer's pharmacies, *SN Supermarket News*, January 6, 2021. <https://www.supermarketnews.com/health-wellness/publix-set-begin-coronavirus-vaccinations-florida>

¹⁴ A list of some of the therapeutics being used is provided in Jeff Craven, "COVID-19 therapeutics tracker," posted January 2022. < https://www.raps.org/news-and-articles/news-articles/2020/3/covid-19-therapeutics-tracker>

¹⁵ "Governor Ron DeSantis Announces Expanded Monoclonal Antibody Access in Florida with New Monoclonal Antibody Centers," August 12, 2021. <https://www.flgov.com/2021/08/12/governor-ron-desantis-announces-expanded-monoclonal-antibody-access-in-florida-with-new-monoclonal-antibody-centers>

¹⁶ Sam Dorman, "Ron DeSantis pressures Biden admin to let states purchase monoclonal antibody treatments: Florida Surgeon General Joseph

Ladapo recently sent Biden administration letter on the issue," *Fox News*, January 3, 2022. <https://www.foxnews.com/politics/ron-desantis-biden-monoclonal-antibodies>

[17] Based on genome sequencing of samples obtained over the four weeks ending January 1, 2022, the CDC estimates these to be 88.9 percent Omicron in Florida, compared to 10 percent for Delta. This would still seem to leave a role for monoclonal antibody therapy in a significant minority of the cases even if they don't work for Omicron. CDC, "Variant Proportions," accessed February 1, 2022. <https://covid.cdc.gov/covid-data-tracker/#variant-proportions>

[18] James Call, "Florida Gov. DeSantis invalidates COVID-19 restrictions statewide, says there's no need 'to be policing people at this point," *USA Today*, May 3, 2021. <https://www.usatoday.com/story/news/nation/2021/05/03/florida-covid-restrictions-gov-ron-desantis-lifts-rules-statewide/4923900001/>

[19] <https://www.aha.org/news/headline/2021-05-13-cdc-ends-indoor-mask-requirements-fully-vaccinated-people>

[20] David Zweig ,"The CDC's Flawed Case for Wearing Masks in School," *The Atlantic*, December 16, 2021. <https://www.theatlantic.com/science/archive/2021/12/mask-guidelines-cdc-walensky/621035/>

[21] Andy Markowitz, "State-by-State Guide to Face Mask Requirements," *AARP*, updated January 26, 2022. <https://www.aarp.org/health/healthy-living/info-2020/states-mask-mandates-coronavirus.html>

[22] The White House, "President Biden Announces New Actions to Protect Americans Against the Delta and Omicron Variants as We Battle COVID-19 this Winter," December 2, 2021. <https://www.whitehouse.gov/briefing-room/statements-releases/2021/12/02/fact-sheet-president-biden-announces-new-actions-to-protect-americans-against-the-delta-and-omicron-variants-as-we-battle-covid-19-this-winter/>

[23] Manoel Nobrega, Renata Opice, Mariana Machado Lauletta, and Christiane Ayello Nobrega, "How face masks can affect school performance," 138, *International Journal of Pediatric Otorhinolaryngology*, November 2020. <https://www.ncbi.nlm.nih.gov/pmc/articles/PMC7462459/>; Goldie Hawn writes poignantly in an op ed about fears of Covid devastating a whole generation of children "whose collective trauma sends them hobbling into adulthood." See Goldie Hawn," COVID trauma is hurting a generation of kids. We've failed them as a nation," *USA Today*, January 26, 2022. <https://www.usatoday.com/story/opinion/2022/01/26/covid-inflicts-childhood-trauma-goldie-hawn/9204091002/>

[24] Jim Saunders, "Florida appeals court casts doubt on school mask case: Judges say DeSantis order 'did not appear to take any action against' parents suing state," *Tallahassee Democrat*, October 27, 2021. <https://www.tallahassee.com/story/news/local/state/2021/10/27/florida-

appeals-court-casts-doubt-school-mask-case-desantis-parents-mandates-judges-order/8576058002/>

[25] Ron DeSantis, "Governor Ron DeSantis Signs Legislation to Protect Florida Jobs," November 18, 2021. <https://www.flgov.com/2021/11/18/governor-ron-desantis-signs-legislation-to-protect-florida-jobs/>

[26] Danielle Ivanov, "Here is what three Florida universities are doing to limit COVID-19 spread this spring," *The Gainesville Sun*, January 7, 2022. <https://www.gainesville.com/story/news/education/campus/2022/01/07/check-out-these-florida-university-covid-19-omicron-policies-spring/9114783002/>

[27] Chris Burt, "State-by-state colleges requiring COVID-19 vaccines, boosters: The complete list of higher education institutions mandating vaccination for the 2021-22 academic year," *UB University Business*, January 2, 2022. <https://universitybusiness.com/state-by-state-look-at-colleges-requiring-vaccines/>

[28] Jorge L. Ortiz, Ryan W. Miller, and Celina Tebor, "Omicron is not that mild: 50,000 to 300,000 more US deaths projected by March: COVID-19 updates," *USA Today*, January 22, 2022. <https://www.usatoday.com/story/news/health/2022/01/18/omicron-final-wave-fauci-nursing-homes-covid-updates/6556051001/>

[29] <https://www.whitehouse.gov/briefing-room/statements-releases/2021/12/02/fact-sheet-president-biden-announces-new-actions-to-protect-americans-against-the-delta-and-omicron-variants-as-we-battle-covid-19-this-winter/>

[30] The most comprehensive study of the impact of lockdowns is a meta-analysis by three economists published by the The Johns Hopkins Institute for Applied Economics, Global Health, and the Study of Business Enterprise. The study considered 34 studies, of which 24 were included in the analysis. Their most general conclusion in a wide-ranging study that includes much useful information on what they call Non-Pharmaceutical Interventions (NFIs) is that while "lockdowns have had little to no public health effects [note: their best estimate was 0.2 percent reduction in Covid-19 mortality], they have imposed enormous economic and social costs where they have been adopted. In consequence, lockdown policies are ill-founded and should be rejected as a pandemic policy instrument." See Jonas Herby, Lars Jonung, and Steve H. Hanke, "A Literature Review and Meta-Analysis of the Effects of Lockdowns on COVID-19 Mortality," *Studies in Applied Economics*, No.200, January 2022. <https://sites.krieger.jhu.edu/iae/files/2022/01/A-Literature-Review-and-Meta-Analysis-of-the-Effects-of-Lockdowns-on-COVID-19-Mortality.pdf>

[31] Timothy Nerozzi, "Biden jokes that Fauci is president, says he sees Fauci more than first lady, Biden says he's 'seen more of Dr. Fauci than I have my wife'," *Fox News*, December 2, 2021. <https://www.foxnews.com/politics/biden-jokes-fauci-president-sees-more-than-first-lady>

[32] "Gov. DeSantis says lockdowns are not an option for Florida as concerns are raised over Omicron variant," *First Coast News ABC*, November 29, 2021. <https://www.firstcoastnews.com/article/news/health/coronavirus/no-lockdowns-for-florida-gov-desantis-promises-as-omicron-variant-raises-national-concern/77-09470ff3-fcb9-4f7a-b4b3-228a97395b79>

[33] Julie Steenhuysen, "Fauci says boosters for all key to U.S. reaching COVID-19 endemic level," Reuters, November 16, 2021. <https://www.reuters.com/world/us/fauci-says-us-can-reach-covid-endemic-level-rather-than-pandemic-next-year-2021-11-16/>

[34] This project is well documented in many papers including Hale et al. (2021) and Hallis et al (2021). And most importantly, all the data is made publicly available on the internet for researchers around the world. <https://www.bsg.ox.ac.uk/research/research-projects/covid-19-government-response-tracker>. It's official academic citation is: Thomas Hale, Noam Angrist, Rafael Goldszmidt, Beatriz Kira, Anna Petherick, Toby Phillips, Samuel Webster, Emily Cameron-Blake, Laura Hallas, Saptarshi Majumdar, and Helen Tatlow. "A global panel database of pandemic policies (Oxford COVID-19 Government Response Tracker)," *Nature Human Behaviour*, (2021). <https://doi.org/10.1038/s41562-021-01079-8>

[35] Laura Hallas, Ariq Hatibie, Rachelle Koch, Saptarshi Majumdar, Monika Pyarali, Andrew Wood, Thomas Hale, "Variation in US states' responses to COVID-19 Ver. 3.0." Working Paper Series, BSG-WP-2020/034, Blavatnik School of Government, Oxford University, May 2021, p.11.

[36] Last data point for the Stringency Index is January 23, 2022.

[37] The states that were classified by Ballotpedia.org as trifecta with a party controlling the governorship, state house, and state senate were attributed to the party in power in these three institutions. The exception was the District of Columbia which Ballotpedia didn't classify as it's not a state and was put in the Democratic column. <https://ballotpedia.org/Partisan_composition_of_state_legislatures>

[38] Hallas et al., *Op. Cit.*, p.50.

[39] Michael Lee, "California to reimpose universal indoor mask mandate," *Fox News*, December 13, 2021.

[40] Jorge L. Ortiz, Ryan W. Miller, and Celina Tebor, *Op. Cit.* <https://www.usatoday.com/story/news/health/2022/01/18/omicron-final-wave-fauci-nursing-homes-covid-updates/6556051001/>

[41] Matthew Conlen, John Keefe, Albert Sun, Lauren Leatherby and Charlie Smart, "How Full Are Hospital I.C.U.s Near You?" *The New York Times*, accessed January 24, 2022. <https://www.nytimes.com/interactive/2020/us/covid-hospitals-near-you.html>

[42] <https://covid.cdc.gov/covid-data-tracker/#datatracker-home>

[43] Miami Herald Editorial Board, "Florida GOP aims to placate anti-vaxxers. DeSantis gets to chest-thump in the end," *Miami Herald*, November 12, 2021. <https://www.miamiherald.com/opinion/editorials/article255675011.html>

44 <https://covid.cdc.gov/covid-data-tracker/#vaccinations_vacc-total-admin-rate-total>

45 Accessed January 29, 2022. <https://www.worldometers.info/coronavirus/country/us/>

46 Ian Schwartz, "Biden Warns: 'Winter Of Severe Illness And Death' For Unvaccinated," *Real Clear Politics*, December 16, 2021. <https://www.realclearpolitics.com/video/2021/12/16/biden_warns_winter_of_severe_illness_and_death_for_unvaccinated.html>

47 Patrick Grady, *Florida Dreams: All About the Amazing Rise of the Sunshine Mega-State* (Amazon, 2019), Ch.27.
<https://www.amazon.com/gp/product/B07LDG9CV9/ref=dbs_a_def_rwt_hsch_vapi_tkin_p1_i0>

48 Mahoney, Emily "Who is Ron DeSantis, the Republican running for Florida governor?" *The Miami Herald*, August 29, 2018.

49 Andrew Gillum's shift leftward is documented in his Tweets over the period. <https://twitter.com/andrewgillum/with_replies>

50 Lawrence Mower, and David Smiley. "New Andrew Gillum documents show FBI agent might have paid for fundraiser dinner." *Tampa Bay Times*. October 26, 2018. <https://www.tampabay.com/florida-politics/buzz/2018/10/26/new-andrew-gillum-documents-show-fbi-agent-might-have-paid-for-fundraiser-dinner/>

51 Ben Ashford and Kayla Brantley, "EXCLUSIVE: This is the gay escort found overdosed on meth in a South Beach hotel room with top Florida Democrat Andrew Gillum - a married father of three who says he was just drunk at a wedding," *Daily Mail*, March 13, 2020.
<https://www.dailymail.co.uk/news/article-8110423/Florida-Democrat-Andrew-Gillum-hotel-room-male-escort-overdosed.html>

52 David Smiley and David Ovalle, "Andrew Gillum found in Miami Beach hotel room with suspected drugs, police say," *Tampa Bay Times*, March 13, 2020.

53 Jacob Ogles, "After Hotel Incident, Florida's Andrew Gillum Comes Out as Bisexual," *The Advocate*, September 14, 2020.

54 Morning Consult and New York Times, "National Tracking Poll," January 14-16, 2022. <https://assets.morningconsult.com/wp-uploads/2022/01/24150429/2201068_topline_PARTNERSHIP_COVID_SURVEY_Adults_v1_SH-1.pdf?campaign_id=9&emc=edit_nn_20220125&instance_id=51211&nl=the-morning&regi_id=22767631&segment_id=80658&te=1&user_id=9ac5df0198ac159de0e542fd62dacd06>; As reported in David Leonhardt ,"Two Covid Americas," *The Morning, The New York Times*, January 25, 2022. <https://messaging-custom-newsletters.nytimes.com/template/oakv2?campaign_id=9&emc=edit_nn_20220125&instance_id=51211&nl=the-morning&productCode=NN&regi_id=22767631&segment_id=80658&te=1&uri

=nyt%3A%2F%2Fnewsletter%2F472591ba-17ee-53fc-83c1-e3923dd33062&user_id=9ac5df0198ac159de0e542fd62dacd06>

55 Jennifer A. Kingson, "Exclusive: $1 billion-plus riot damage is most expensive in insurance history," *Axios*, September 16, 2020. <https://www.axios.com/riots-cost-property-damage-276c9bcc-a455-4067-b06a-66f9db4cea9c.html>

56 Wikipedia, "George Floyd protests in Florida," accessed December 13, 2021. <https://en.wikipedia.org/wiki/George_Floyd_protests_in_Florida>

57 Mike Cugno, "Looters Strike Bayside Marketside As Demonstrators Clash With Miami Police," *4 CBS Miami*, May 30, 2020. <https://miami.cbslocal.com/2020/05/30/looters-bayside-marketplace-miami-protest-violence-george-floyd/>

58 <https://twitter.com/govrondesantis/status/1267562102249721856?lang=da>

59 <https://crime-data-explorer.app.cloud.gov/pages/explorer/crime/crime-trend>

60 *Ibid*.

61 Ibid.

62 Miami Dade Police Department, Part 1 Crimes YTD Comparison – Automated, Date Range Jan 1, 2021 - Dec 12, 2021. <https://www.miamidade.gov/police/library/part-1-crimes-ytd-comparison.pdf>

63 Audrey Conklin, "At least 16 cities see record homicides in 2021," *Fox News*, December 18, 2021. <https://www.foxnews.com/us/cities-record-homicides-2021>

64 German Lopez, "Examining the Spike in Murders," *New York Times*, January 18, 2022. <https://www.nytimes.com/2022/01/18/briefing/crime-surge-homicides-us.html>

65 Mark Moore, "DeSantis wants to pay unvaccinated cops $5K to relocate to Florida," *New York Post*, October 25, 2021. <https://nypost.com/2021/10/25/desantis-wants-to-pay-unvaccinated-cops-5k-to-relocate-to-florida/>

66 Associated Press, "A Judge Has Blocked The 'Anti-Riot' Law Passed In Florida After George Floyd Protests," September 9, 2021. <https://www.npr.org/2021/09/09/1035687247/florida-anti-riot-law-ron-desantis-george-floyd-black-lives-matter-protests>

67 California Courts, "Proposition 47 FAQs," Updated November 16, 2016. <https://www.courts.ca.gov/documents/Prop47FAQs.pdf>

68 FOX Business Staff, "Florida won't become California, Minnesota with new crime initiative, AG Moody says," *Fox Business*, December 2, 2021. <https://www.foxbusiness.com/politics/florida-wont-become-california-minnesota-new-crime-initiative-ag-moody>

69 Ian Schwartz, "SF Mayor London Breed Announces Crackdown, Policies 'Less Tolerant Of The Bullshit That Has Destroyed Our City'," *RealClearPolitics*,

December 15, 2021. <https://www.realclearpolitics.com/video/2021/12/15/sf_mayor_london_breed_announces_crackdown_policies_less_tolerant_of_the_bullshit_that_has_destroyed_our_city.html>

70 U.S. Census Bureau, "New Vintage 2021 Population Estimates Available for the Nation, States and Puerto Rico," Release Number CB21-208, December 21, 2021. <https://www.census.gov/newsroom/press-releases/2021/2021-population-estimates.html>

71 Office of Economic & Demographic Research, "Demographic Estimating Conference: Florida Demographic Forecast," December 13, 2021. <http://edr.state.fl.us/Content/conferences/population/index.cfm>

72 Conor Skelding, "The sixth borough: Florida state records quantify defections from NY," *New York Post*, May 15, 2021. <https://nypost.com/2021/05/15/florida-records-quantify-number-of-defections-from-ny/>

73 Again Ballotpedia.org was used to classify the states by party. <https://ballotpedia.org/Partisan_composition_of_state_legislatures>

74 <https://www.census.gov/data/tables/time-series/demo/popest/2020s-state-total.html>

75 Gregor Aisch, Robert Gebeloff and Kevin Quealy, "Where We Came From and Where We Went, State by State." *New York Times*. UPDATED August 19, 2014. <https://www.nytimes.com/interactive/2014/08/13/upshot/where-people-in-each-state-were-born.html>

76 "U-Haul Growth Index: Texas is the No. 1 Growth State of 2021," January 3, 2022. <https://www.uhaul.com/Articles/About/U-Haul-Growth-Index-Texas-Is-The-No-1-Growth-State-Of-2021-26380/>

77 Karol Markowicz, "I am leaving New York City for Florida. I never thought I would," *Fox News*, December 7, 2021. <https://www.foxnews.com/opinion/leaving-new-york-city-florida-karol-markowicz>

78 <https://www.census.gov/data/tables/time-series/demo/popest/2020s-state-total.html>

79 The U.S. Government reported that almost 2 million people illegally entered the country in the twelve months ending September 30, 2021. See Julian Resendiz, "U.S. officials come across nearly 2 million unauthorized migrants in FY 2021," October 22, 2021. <https://www.borderreport.com/hot-topics/immigration/u-s-officials-come-across-nearly-2-million-unauthorized-migrants-in-fy-2021/> As difficult as this may be to swallow, the Census Bureau claims that it includes "unauthorized residents" in resident population counts. <https://www.census.gov/topics/public-sector/congressional-apportionment/about/faqs.html>

80 <https://www.census.gov/data/tables/time-series/demo/popest/2020s-state-total.html>

[81] Virginia Aabram, "'I will send them to Delaware': DeSantis threatens to remove migrants flown to Florida by Biden administration," *Washington Examiner*, November 11, 2021. <https://www.washingtonexaminer.com/news/i-will-send-them-to-delaware-desantis-threatens-to-remove-migrants-flown-to-florida-by-biden-administration>

[82] <https://www.youtube.com/watch?v=pP9Bto5lOEQ>

[83] Patricia Mazzei, "Miami Embraces Cuba Protests: 'I Never Thought That This Day Would Come'," *The New York Times*, July 17, 2021. <https://www.nytimes.com/2021/07/17/us/cuba-protests-miami-florida.html>

[84] Brian Ellsworth and Marc Frank, "Cuban Americans rally in Miami while protest plans fizzle in Havana," *Reuters*, November 14, 2021. <https://www.reuters.com/world/americas/cuban-americans-rally-miami-support-dissidents-who-plan-protests-cuba-2021-11-14/>

[85] Archipiélago. <https://www.facebook.com/groups/870004956941838>

[86] Jon Lee Anderson, "Obama and Raúl Castro's Awkward Embrace in Cuba," *New Yorker*, March 22, 2016. <https://www.newyorker.com/news/news-desk/obama-and-raul-castros-awkward-embrace-in-cuba>

[87] The White House, "Charting a New Course on Cuba." <https://obamawhitehouse.archives.gov/issues/foreign-policy/cuba>; Doug Palmer, "Obama relaxes trade restrictions with Cuba," *Politico*, October 14, 2016. <https://www.politico.com/story/2016/10/obama-cuba-trade-openings-expanded-229789>; Matt Spetalnick, Daniel Trotta, Jeff Mason, "Obama in Cuba on historic visit," *Reuters*, March 26, 2016. <https://www.reuters.com/article/us-usa-cuba/obama-in-cuba-on-historic-visit-idUSKCN0WM04H>; Dan Roberts, "Obama lands in Cuba as first US president to visit in nearly a century," *The Guardian*, March 21, 2016. <https://www.theguardian.com/world/2016/mar/20/barack-obama-cuba-visit-us-politics-shift-public-opinion-diplomacy>

[88] BBC News, "Cuba denounces Trump's policy rollback," June 17, 2017. <https://www.bbc.com/news/world-us-canada-40311287>

[89] Matthew Lee, and Joshua Goodman, Associated Press, "Trump hits Cuba with new sanctions in waning days," *PBS News Hour*, January 11, 2021. <https://www.pbs.org/newshour/politics/trump-hits-cuba-with-new-terrorism-sanctions-in-waning-days>

[90] Black Lives Matter, *Statement*, July 14, 2021. <https://www.instagram.com/p/CRU5kYYp-UU/?utm_medium=copy_link>

[91] Bendixen & Amandi International, "Survey of Florida Cuban-American Voters March 2021," <https://www.politico.com/states/f/?id=00000178-387f-dc18-af7d-fc7f84040000>

[92] <https://apps.bea.gov/itable/iTable.cfm?ReqID=70&step=1#reqid=70&step=1&isuri=1>

⁹³ *Ibid*.

⁹⁴ The specific monetary and fiscal measures introduced to support the economy during Covid are well summarized in Investopedia, U.S. Covid-19 Stimulus and Relief, Updated December 30, 2021. <https://www.investopedia.com/government-stimulus-efforts-to-fight-the-covid-19-crisis-4799723> Untangling the differential impact of this rat's nest of monetary and fiscal programs on the different states economies is well beyond the capability of this, and probably even, any study given the current state of economic science.

⁹⁵ <https://apps.bea.gov/itable/iTable.cfm?ReqID=70&step=1#reqid=70&step=1&isuri=1>

⁹⁶ <https://beta.bls.gov/covid-dashboard/home.htm>

⁹⁷ *Ibid*.

⁹⁸<https://data.bls.gov/timeseries/LASST120000000000003?amp%253bdata_tool=XGtable&output_view=data&include_graphs=true>

⁹⁹ <https://www.bls.gov/web/laus/laumstrk.htm#laumstrk.f.p>

¹⁰⁰ Wiji Arulampalam, Paul Gregg, Mary Gregory, "Unemployment Scarring," *The Economic Journal*, Volume 111, Issue 475, November 2001, Pp. F577–F584.

¹⁰¹ Asfiya Kidwai and Zain Sarwar, "Psychological Impacts of Unemployment –Evidence from the Literature," *Review of Integrative Business Economics Research*, Vol 4(3), (2015). <file:///C:/Users/P_Gra/Downloads/riber_b15-144_141-152.pdf>

¹⁰² The maximum regular unemployment insurance benefit in Florida (called Reemployment Assistance) was only $275 per week. The Pandemic Unemployment Compensation, which was paid in addition, was 218 per cent higher, making for a total of $875 per week. This is way more than most people can expect to earn in a low-wage economy like Florida. Consequently, it should be obvious why it was difficult to get workers who were eligible for these benefits. See Florida Department of Revenue, "Employer Guide to Reemployment Assistance Benefits," accessed February 1, 2022. <https://floridarevenue.com/forms_library/current/rt800001.pdf>

¹⁰³ Center on Budget and Policy Priorities, "Policy Basics: Unemployment Insurance." <https://www.cbpp.org/research/economy/unemployment-insurance>

¹⁰⁴Thomas Mates and Erik von Ancken, "Florida announces end to federally funded boost to unemployment benefits," *ClickOrlando.com*, May 24, 2021. <https://www.clickorlando.com/news/local/2021/05/24/florida-announces-end-to-federally-funded-boost-to-unemployment-benefits/>

¹⁰⁵ <https://www.cbpp.org/research/economy/how-many-weeks-of-unemployment-compensation-are-available>

¹⁰⁶ Office of Economic and Demographic Research, State of Florida, "Executive Summary, Revenue Estimating Conference for the General Revenue

Fund & Financial Outlook Statement," August 14, 2020, p.1. <http://edr.state.fl.us/content/conferences/generalrevenue/archives/200814gr.pdf>

[107] Governor Ron DeSantis, *Fiscal Year 2020-21 Budget: Florida Leads*, June 2, 2021, p.1. <https://www.flgov.com/wp-content/uploads/2021/06/FY-21-22-Budget-Highlights-6.2.21-FINAL.pdf>

[108] World Population Review, "Debt by State 2021. <https://worldpopulationreview.com/state-rankings/debt-by-state>

[109] All the states' credit ratings from the three agencies, Fitch, Moody's, and Standard & Poor's are provided in: California State Treasurer, Public Finance Division, "California's Current Credit Ratings," accessed January 23, 2022. <https://www.treasurer.ca.gov/ratings/current.asp>

[110] Brian Chappatta, "Goldman Sachs Goes All-In on Florida as Wall Street South," *Bloomberg Opinion*, June 14, 2021. <https://www.bloomberg.com/opinion/articles/2021-06-14/goldman-sachs-goes-all-in-on-florida-as-wall-street-south>

[111] Avery Hartmans, "3 top execs at hedge fund Elliott Management have put their New York apartments up for sale as the firm moves to Miami, *Business Insider*, February 24, 2021. <https://www.businessinsider.com/elliott-management-execs-selling-new-york-homes-photos-2021-2>

[112] Josh Kosman, "Carl Icahn has officially ditched NYC for Florida," *New York* Post, August 12, 2020. <https://nypost.com/2020/08/12/carl-icahn-has-officially-ditched-nyc-for-florida/>

[113] Icahn Enterprises LP, *Annual Report 2020*, p.1. <https://www.ielp.com/static-files/dd7b34ea-4bf8-433e-a969-b25ca1218e4b>

[114] "Blackstone Reports Fourth Quarter and Full Year 2020 Results," January 27, 2021, p.1. <https://www.blackstone.com/wp-content/uploads/sites/2/2021/01/Blackstone4Q20EarningsPressRelease.pdf>

[115] Grace Dean, "Tech jobs, sun, and no income tax: experts explain why Florida is poised to keep growing even after the pandemic," *Business Insider*, May 21, 2021. <https://www.businessinsider.com/florida-growth-jobs-economy-population-new-york-pandemic-employment-miami-2021-4>

[116] Lidia Dinkova, Blackstone buys MiamiCentral office buildings for $230M," *The Real Deal*, March 19, 2021. <https://therealdeal.com/miami/2021/03/19/blackstone-buys-miamicentral-office-buildings-for-230m/>

[117] David Gura, "Miami wants to become crypto's financial capital. New York's response? Bring it on," *NPR*, December 25, 2021. <https://www.npr.org/2021/12/25/1063578188/miami-wants-to-become-cryptos-financial-capital-new-yorks-response-bring-it-on>

[118] Paul Vigna, "Blockchain.com Raises $300 Million as Investors Find Other Ways Into Bitcoin," *Wall Street Journal*, March 24, 2021. <https://www.wsj.com/articles/blockchain-com-raises-300-million-as-investors-find-other-ways-into-bitcoin-11616576413>>

[119] David Gura, *Op. Cit.*
[120] Mike Schneider, "Disney World opened 50 years ago; these workers never left," *AP News*," September 29, 2021. <https://apnews.com/article/business-lifestyle-entertainment-travel-arts-and-entertainment-071c80ae6c0dabe6e1afbc3b59240131>; *NBC12*, Brittany Melling, "How Much Land Does Disney Own?," *.askBamLand*, July 23, 2021. <https://www.askbamland.com/post/how-much-land-does-disney-own>
[121] Megan duBois, "Disney Is Moving 2000 Jobs To Central Florida In An Unprecedented Uprooting", *Forbes*, July 19, 2021. <https://www.forbes.com/sites/megandubois/2021/07/19/disney-is-moving-2000-jobs-to-central-florida-in-an-unprecedented-uprooting/?sh=66adcc58249d>; "Disney to relocate 2,000 jobs from California to Florida at Orlando's Lake Nona community," *FOX 35 News*, July 15, 2021. <https://www.fox13news.com/news/disney-confirms-plan-to-relocate-2000-jobs-to-orlandos-lake-nona>
[122] Amy Krieger, "Disney Purchases Nearly 60 Acres of Land for Planned Lake Nona Campus," *Moving to Orlando*, September 18, 2021. <https://movingtoorlando.com/disney/disney-purchases-nearly-60-acres-of-land-for-planned-lake-nona-campus/>
[123] Marco Santana, "KPMG unveils $450M, high-tech Lake Nona training center with 800 'hotel' rooms," *Orlando Sentinel*, January 15, 2020. <https://www.orlandosentinel.com/business/os-bz-kpmg-lake-nona-training-center-20200114-gpkijlp23zfwvniopmvjluet64-story.html>
[124] Jeff Ostrowski, "Carrier makes it official: Headquarters is in Palm Beach Gardens," *The Palm Beach Post*, March 4, 2020. <https://www.palmbeachpost.com/story/business/2020/03/04/carrier-makes-it-official-headquarters-is-in-palm-beach-gardens/112243044/>
[125] Florida Inventors Hall of Fame. <https://floridainvents.org/john-gorrie/?doing_wp_cron=1643582499.5371139049530029296875>
[126] Lee Ohanian, "Leaving California: Elon Musk Moves To Texas And Takes Tesla With Him," *Hoover Institution*, October 14, 2021. <https://www.hoover.org/research/leaving-california-elon-musk-moves-texas-and-takes-tesla-him>
[127] Alex Viega, "Elon Musk says Tesla will move HQ from California to Texas," *Associated Press*, October 7, 2021. <https://apnews.com/article/technology-business-palo-alto-elon-musk-austin-7a9b375a5b69c25564c9ae4dc4fba64e>
[128] Laine Doss, "Carbone's Major Food Group to Build Miami's Tallest Building," *Miami New Times*, December 2, 2021. <https://www.miaminewtimes.com/restaurants/major-food-group-to-build-miamis-tallest-building-13440872>
[129] Nicole Lopez-Alvar, "Wynwood's new venue 'The Oasis' set to become Miami's newest culinary, retail, and nightlife destination," *Local10.com*, Updated: March 30, 2021.

<https://www.local10.com/entertainment/2021/03/29/wynwoods-new-outdoor-concert-venue-the-oasis-is-set-to-become-the-newest-culinary-retail-and-nightlife-destination-in-miami/>

[130] Josh Kosman, "Subway Restaurants is making move south to Miami from Connecticut," *New York Post*, March 11, 2021 <https://nypost.com/2021/03/11/subway-restaurants-moving-move-south-to-miami-from-connecticut/>

[131] Ben Coley, "Subway to Move Some of its Business to Miami: The transition could lead to more layoffs, reports say," *Fast Food*, March 15, 2021. <https://www.qsrmagazine.com/fast-food/subway-move-some-its-business-miami>

[132] "Civix's New Center of Excellence, August 5, 2020. <https://gocivix.com/news/center-of-excellence-is-advancing-innovation-in-govtech/>

[133] "Sonesta to Establish New Corporate Offices in Downtown Orlando: Eighth Largest Hotel Company to Open New Orlando Office in June 2021," March 25, 2021. <https://www.sonesta.com/sonesta-to-establish-new-corporate-offices-downtown-orlando>

[134] "The Fortune 500: Special Section," *Fortune*, Volume 183, No. 3, June/July 2021.

[135] Jay Cridlin, "Largo's Tech Data merging with Synnex in $7.2 billion deal," *Tampa Bay Times*, March 22, 2021, <https://www.tampabay.com/news/business/2021/03/22/largos-tech-data-merging-with-synnex-in-72-billion-deal/#:~:text=The%20merger%20follows%20Tech%20Data's,private%20equity%20firm%20last%20summer.&text=Less%20than%20a%20year%20after,is%20preparing%20for%20a%20merger.>; Jay Cridlin, "Largo's Tech Data completes $8.3 billion merger, becomes TD Synnex," *Tampa Bay Times*, September 2, 2021, <https://www.tampabay.com/news/business/2021/09/01/largos-tech-data-completes-83-billion-merger-becomes-td-synnex/>

The merger with California's Synnex Corp. will remake one of Tampa Bay's largest companies.

[136] Governor Ron DeSantis, "Florida Tourism Continues to Surpass Pre-Pandemic Levels," Press release on February 15, 2022. <https://www.flgov.com/2022/02/15/florida-tourism-continues-to-surpass-pre-pandemic-levels/>

[137] VisitFlorida, "Florida Visitor Estimates and Travel Industry Trend Indicators," Released February 15, 2022. <https://visitflorida.app.box.com/s/yybwlayqp5ul95851p1vobhwjpsxr2cr>

[138] VisitFlorida, *Ibid*.

[139] VisitFlorida, *Ibid*.

[140] Sophia Harris, "Ottawa advises Canadians not to travel abroad," *CBC News*, March 15, 2020. <https://www.cbc.ca/news/business/government-travel-advisory-coronavirus-insurance-1.5498275>

[141] Prime Minister of Canada Justin Trudeau, "Prime Minister announces temporary border agreement with the United States," March 20, 2020. <https://pm.gc.ca/en/news/news-releases/2020/03/20/prime-minister-announces-temporary-border-agreement-united-states>

[142] Kait Bolongaro, "Canada Sets Aug. 9 Border Opening for Vaccinated U.S. Visitors," *Bloomberg*, July 19, 2021. <https://www.bloomberg.com/news/articles/2021-07-19/canada-will-open-border-to-fully-vaccinated-u-s-visitors-aug-9>

[143] Sophia Harris, "The U.S. land border is open. Here's what you need to know," *CBC News*, November 8, 2021. <https://www.cbc.ca/news/business/u-s-land-border-open-vaccinated-1.6233944>

[144] Sophia Harris, "Canadian snowbirds question why land border is still closed as they prepare to fly to U.S., ship their RVs, *CBC News*, October 3, 2021. <https://www.cbc.ca/news/business/snowbirds-u-s-land-border-1.6193875>

[145] Visit Florida, "Florida Visitor Estimates," accessed January 23, 2022. <https://www.visitflorida.org/resources/research/>

[146] "'Tremendous pent-up demand': U.S. border reopens to Canadian land travelers," *Reuters*, November 9, 2021. <https://www.reuters.com/world/us/tremendous-pent-up-demand-us-border-reopens-canadian-land-travelers-2021-11-08/>

[147] Josh Freed, "Florida feels like another planet compared with Quebec," *Montreal Gazette*, January 22, 2022. <https://montrealgazette.com/news/local-news/josh-freed-florida-feels-like-another-planet-compared-with-quebec> Floridians may detect similarities between the style of Freed and our own native humorist Craig Pitman.

[148] Josh Freed, "Column teasing Floridians about COVID strikes angry chord," *Montreal Gazette*, January 22, 2022. < https://montrealgazette.com/opinion/columnists/josh-freed-column-teasing-floridians-about-covid-strikes-angry-chord?__vfz=medium%3Dstandalone_content_recirculation_with_ads>

[149] Staff Reporter, "Trucker convoy: Police report no injuries, 'no incidents of violence' after first day of protest," *Ottawa Citizen*, January 29, 2022. <https://ottawacitizen.com/news/local-news/trucker-convoy-more-trucks-expected-on-saturday-traffic-impacts-expected-to-worsen>; John Paul Trasker, "Thousands opposed to COVID-19 rules converge on Parliament Hill," *CBC News*, January 29, 2022. <https://www.cbc.ca/news/politics/truck-convoy-protest-some-key-players-1.6332312> While these articles are good example of the negative coverage provided by the Canadian national media to anything or anyone dissenting from the official Covid consensus, they does convey the extent of the protest and the strong opposition of the participants against the Covid shutdowns in Canada.

[150] Associated Press, "Some Original Staffers Say They're Still Happy To Work At Disney World After 50 Years," *NPR*, September 28, 2021.

<https://www.npr.org/2021/09/28/1041270317/some-original-staffers-say-theyre-still-happy-to-work-at-disney-world-after-50-y>

[151] Curtis Tate, "Disney lost nearly $5 billion while theme parks were closed due to coronavirus," *USA Today*, August 4, 2020. <https://www.usatoday.com/story/travel/2020/08/04/disneys-theme-park-coronavirus-closures-result-hit-3-5-billion/3292766001/>

[152] Data from AECM/TEA, *2020 Theme Index, Museum Index Global Attractions Attendance Report*, p. 12. <https://aecom.com/wp-content/uploads/documents/reports/AECOM-Theme-Index-2020.pdf>

[153] Tribune News Service, "Disney World boosts park capacity, loosens mask rules: Masks are now only required in indoor spaces at the Orlando parks," *Tampa Bay Times*, May 17, 2021. <https://www.tampabay.com/life-culture/entertainment/theme-parks/2021/05/17/disney-world-boosts-park-capacity-loosens-mask-rules/>

[154] Jenna Saxton, "Disney World Updates Mask Policy For Outdoor Attractions and More," *AllEars*, August 18, 2021. <https://allears.net/2021/08/18/news-disney-world-updates-mask-policy-for-outdoor-attractions-and-more/>

[155] CNN News Staff, "Disney World halts COVID-19 vaccine mandate for employees following change in Florida law," *KSNBLocal4*, November 22, 2021. <https://www.ksnblocal4.com/2021/11/22/disney-world-halts-covid-19-vaccine-mandate-employees-following-change-florida-law/>

[156] Tom Bricker, "Massive Crowds for MLK Weekend 2022 at Disney World," *Disney Tourist Blog*, accessed January 24, 2022. <https://www.disneytouristblog.com/crowds-mlk-day-weekend-disney-world/>

[157] Frank Pallotta, "Disneyland closes because of the coronavirus outbreak," *CNN Business*, March 12, 2020. <https://www.cnn.com/2020/03/12/media/disneyland-close-coronavirus/index.html>

[158] Grace Kay, "Disneyland and other California theme parks just returned to full capacity — here's what is changing," *Business Insider*, June 15, 2021. <https://www.businessinsider.com/disneyland-california-universal-theme-parks-return-full-capacity-june-15-2021-5>

[159] Business Research & Economic Advisors, "The Economic Contribution of the International Cruise Industry in the United States in 2019," November 2020. <https://cruising.org/-/media/research-updates/research/2019-usa-cruise-eis.ashx>

[160] Wikipedia, "COVID-19 pandemic on cruise ships." <https://en.wikipedia.org/wiki/COVID-19_pandemic_on_cruise_ships#World_Dream>

[161] CDC, "Cruise Ship Travel During COVID-19, updated Jan. 5, 2022. <https://www.cdc.gov/coronavirus/2019-ncov/travelers/cruise-travel-during-

covid19.html#:~:text=The%20chance%20of%20getting%20COVID,worldwide%2C%20regardless%20of%20vaccination%20status.>

[162] CDC, "CDC COVID-19 Orders for Cruise Ships," accessed January 26, 2022. <https://www.cdc.gov/quarantine/cruise/covid19-cruiseships.html>

[163] Aaron Saunders and Chris Gray Faust, "Pressure on CDC Grows, As Cruise Lines Plan More International Restarts," *Cruisecritic*, March 25, 2021. <https://www.cruisecritic.com/news/5988/>

[164] Robert McGillivray, "Why Florida Needs to Fight for Cruises to Resume," *CruiseHive*, April 9, 2021. <https://www.cruisehive.com/why-florida-needs-to-fight-for-cruises-to-resume/49469>

[165] "Pete Williams, "Appeals court blocks CDC Covid restrictions, allowing cruises to resume from Florida," *NBC News*, July 23, 2021. <https://www.nbcnews.com/politics/supreme-court/florida-asks-supreme-court-let-cruise-ships-sail-again-n1274884>

[166] CDC, *Op. Cit.* <https://www.cdc.gov/quarantine/cruise/covid19-cruiseships.html>

[167] Carolyn Crist, "First U.S. Cruise Ship Sets Sail After 15 Months," *WebMD*, June 28, 2021. <https://www.webmd.com/lung/news/20210627/first-u-s-cruise-ship-sets-sail-after-15-months>

[168] Business Research & Economic Advisors, *Op. Cit.*, p.12. <https://cruising.org/-/media/research-updates/research/2019-usa-cruise-eis.ashx>

[169] Rebekah Castor, Cruise industry tries to stay afloat during omicron surge, *Fox News*, January 11, 2022. <https://www.foxnews.com/us/cruise-industry-tries-to-stay-afloat-during-omicron-surge>

[170] Rebekah Castor, *Op. Cit.* <https://www.foxnews.com/us/cruise-industry-tries-to-stay-afloat-during-omicron-surge>; Royal Caribbean, "Cruise Health and Travel Alerts," updated January 29, 2022. <https://www.royalcaribbean.com/cruise-ships/itinerary-updates>

[171] Jesus Jiménez, "Cruise Has Surprise Ending After Judge Orders Ship Seized Over Debts," The New York Times, January 23, 2022. <https://www.nytimes.com/2022/01/23/us/crystal-cruises-ship-diverted.html>

[172] Freddie Mac, 30-Year Fixed Rate Mortgage Average in the United States [MORTGAGE30US], retrieved from FRED, Federal Reserve Bank of St. Louis, January 19, 2022. <https://fred.stlouisfed.org/series/MORTGAGE30US>

[173] Retrieved from St. Louis Federal Reserve Bank, FRED, January 16, 2022. <https://fred.stlouisfed.org/series/FLBPPRIVSA>

[174] U.S. Federal Housing Finance Agency. Retrieved from St. Louis Federal Reserve Bank, FRED, January 16, 2022. <https://geofred.stlouisfed.org/map/?th=ylgn&cc=5&rc=false&im=fractile&sb&lng=-82.27&lat=56.37&zm=3&sl&sv&sti=942&rt=state&at=Not%20Seasonally%20Adjusted,%20Quarterly,%20Index%201980:Q1%3D100,%20no_period_desc&fq=Quarterly&dt=2021-07-01&am=Average&un=lin>

[175] Retrieved from St. Louis Federal Reserve Bank, FRED, January 16, 2022. <https://fred.stlouisfed.org/series/FLSTHPI>

[176] Gregg Logan and Karl Pischke, "The Top-Selling Master-Planned Communities of Mid-Year 2021," July 12, 2021. <https://www.rclco.com/publication/the-top-selling-master-planned-communities-of-mid-year-2021/>

[177] Asher Wildman, "New Disney campus expected to create housing boom in Lake Nona," *Spectrum News13*, July 16, 2021. <https://www.mynews13.com/fl/orlando/news/2021/07/16/new-disney-campus-expected-to-create-housing-boom-in-lake-nona>

[178] <https://babcockranch.com/>

[179] See Patrick Grady, *Op. Cit.*, chapter 16.

[180] Brianna Crane and Ben Montgomery "User's guide: Everything you need to know about Water Street Tampa," *Axios Tampa Bay*, Updated October 13, 2021. <https://www.axios.com/local/tampa-bay/2021/10/13/users-guide-everything-know-about-water-street-tampa>

[181] <https://waterstreettampa.com/>

[182] Earle Kimel, "Allegiant Air Sunseeker Resort on track: Summer groundbreaking expected for 25-plus acre resort in Punta Gorda," *Herald-Tribune*, April 6, 2018, <https://www.heraldtribune.com/story/news/local/sarasota/2018/04/06/allegiant-air-sunseeker-resort-on-track-in-charlotte-county/12801752007/>

[183] Erika Jackson and Jack Lowenstein, "Allegiant halts Sunseeker construction; workers say they were unaware," *Wink News*, March 18, 2020. <https://www.winknews.com/2020/03/18/allegiant-halts-sunseeker-construction-workers-say-they-were-unaware/>

[184] "Allegiant halts Sunseeker project indefinitely in Charlotte Harbor," Wink News, May 18, 2020. <https://www.winknews.com/2020/05/18/allegiant-halts-sunseeker-project-indefinitely-in-charlotte-harbor/>

[185] Allegiant Press Release, "Sunseeker Resorts Resumes Construction Of Charlotte Harbor Development," August 3, 2021. <https://ir.allegiantair.com/news-releases/news-release-details/sunseeker-resorts-resumes-construction-charlotte-harbor>

[186] Mark Gordon, "$510 million transformational resort project gets a reboot," Business Observer, August 12, 2021. <https://www.businessobserverfl.com/article/dollar510-million-transformational-resort-project-gets-a-reboot>

[187] Ron Hurtibise, "Future unclear for planned $4 billion mega-mall in Florida," *South Florida Sun-Sentinel*, September 20, 2021. <https://www.msn.com/en-us/money/realestate/will-american-dream-miami-mega-mall-ever-become-reality/ar-AAOzNr3>

[188] "These Are The 21 New Miami Towers That Will Be Under Construction In 2021," January 7, 2021. <https://www.thenextmiami.com/these-are-the-21-new-miami-towers-that-will-be-under-construction-in-2021/>

[189] Rob Wile, "Miami's tech sector posts banner year in 2021. Here are the top 8 developments," *Miami Herald*, December 19, 2021. <https://www.miamiherald.com/article256593806.html>

[190] <https://apps.bea.gov/itable/iTable.cfm?ReqID=70&step=1>

[191] <https://apps.bea.gov/itable/iTable.cfm?ReqID=70&step=1>

[192] Jonas Herby, Lars Jonung, and Steve H. Hanke, *Op. Cit.* <https://sites.krieger.jhu.edu/iae/files/2022/01/A-Literature-Review-and-Meta-Analysis-of-the-Effects-of-Lockdowns-on-COVID-19-Mortality.pdf>

[193] Ronn Blitzer, "DeSantis jokes about Dems from strict COVID states visiting Florida after AOC spotted maskless in Miami: 'I mean, Congress people, mayors, governors, I mean you name it'," *Fox News*, January 4, 2022. <https://www.foxnews.com/politics/desantis-jokes-about-dems-from-strict-states-visiting-fl-after-aoc-spotted-maskless-in-miami>

[194] For a more detailed discussion of the environmental challenges resulting from population growth, see Patrick Grady, *Florida Dreams: All About the Amazing Rise of the Sunshine Mega-State* (Amazon, 2019), chapter 26. <https://www.amazon.com/gp/product/B07LDG9CV9/ref=dbs_a_def_rwt_hsch_vapi_tkin_p1_i0>

[195] Jessica Meszaros, "Tampa Bay Algae Blooms Could Be Fed By Piney Point Wastewater," *WUSF Public Media - WUSF 89.7*, June 11, 2021. <https://wusfnews.wusf.usf.edu/environment/2021-06-11/tampa-bay-algae-blooms-could-be-fed-by-piney-point-wastewater>

[196] Jesse Mendoza, Piney Point springs a leak, again, but Florida officials are not concerned," *Sarasota Herald-Tribune*, January 22, 2022. <https://www.heraldtribune.com/story/news/local/manatee/2022/01/13/piney-point-fertilizer-plant-springs-leak-again-florida-officials-not-concerned/6510326001/>

[197] Joseph Choi, "Fauci says 'we're going to have to start living with COVID'," *The Hill*, November 28, 2021. <https://thehill.com/homenews/sunday-talk-shows/583269-fauci-were-going-to-have-to-start-living-with-covid>

[198] John Paul Tasker, "Antivirals could be a pandemic game-changer — and they could be in Canada soon, *CBC News*, January 14, 2022. <https://www.cbc.ca/news/politics/game-changing-covid-antivirals-canada-soon-1.6314214>

[199] Even using data available on January 1, 2020, before Covid hit, Florida was ranked as the second freest state in the country according to the Cato Institute's index of personal and economic freedom. William P. Ruger and Jason Sorens, *Freedom in the 50 States: An Index of Personal and Economic Freedom*, (Washington: Cato Institute, 2021). <https://www.freedominthe50states.org/>

[200] Tyler O'Neil, "DeSantis takes aim at CRT training in schools and corporate America," Fox News, December 15, 2021. <https://www.foxnews.com/politics/desantis-critical-race-theory-training-schools-corporate-america>
[201] < https://www.justice.gov/ag/page/file/1438986/download>
[202] <https://www.governor.virginia.gov/executive-actions/>

www.ingramcontent.com/pod-product-compliance
Lightning Source LLC
Chambersburg PA
CBHW071520220526
45472CB00003B/1099